What Is the Church?

formerly: The Church: God's People

Bruce L. Shelley

This book is designed for your personal reading pleasure and profit. It is also designed for group study. A leader's guide with Victor Multiuse Transparency Masters is available from your local Christian bookstore or from the publisher.

VICTOR

BOOKS a division of SP Publications, Inc.
WHEATON. ILLINOIS 60187

Offices also in
Whitby, Ontario, Canada
Amersham-on-the-Hill, Bucks, England

About the Author

Bruce L. Shelley is professor of church history at Conservative Baptist Theological Seminary, Denver. He is a graduate of Columbia Bible College (B.A.), Fuller Theological Seminary (M.Div.), and University of Iowa (Ph.D.). He has written for numerous Christian publications and is also author of *Four Marks of a Total Christian* (Victor).

Other books in the "Basic Doctrine Series":

Who Is Jesus? by Bruce A. Demarest
What Is Man? by Leslie B. Flynn
Is the Bible Reliable? by Robert L. Saucy

Bible quotations are from the *King James Version*. Other quotations are from the *New International Version: New Testament* (NIV), © 1973, The New York Bible Society; the *New American Standard Bible* (NASB), © 1960, 1962, 1963, 1968, 1971, 1972, 1973, The Lockman Foundation, La Habra, California; *The Living Bible* (LB), Tyndale House Publishers; the *Revised Standard Version* (RSV), © 1946 and 1952, The Division of Christian Education, National Council of the Churches of Christ in the U.S.A.

Library of Congress Catalog Card Number: 82-61575
ISBN: 0-88207-105-X

VICTOR BOOKS
A division of SP Publications, Inc.
P.O. Box 1825 • Wheaton, Illinois 60187

Contents

Preface

"Christ . . . loved the church and gave Himself for it" (Eph. 5:25). Every Christian needs to come to terms with that text. If Jesus loved the church, so should I.

As we look about us, we find churches and we find churches. Many of today's religious organizations cannot call for our devotion and obedience, for to obey them would be to disobey the Gospel. They simply are not adequate expressions of the grace and power of God.

I intend, therefore, no blanket approval of every religious body today that claims the title *church*. In this book, we argue that institutional forms alone do not make the church. In the New Testament, the church can only be understood as a product of the Gospel of God's supernatural grace. This is the kind of church I am talking about in these pages.

On the other hand, I do not think the Bible supports the maneuver of many evangelical Christians. In their rejection of today's corruptions of the church, described in the New Testament, many evangelicals attempt to argue that the "true" church is "not institutional." I don't think the Bible supports that idea. My reasons are in the pages of this book.

Before I plunge in, I want to express my appreciation to some of my helpers. My dependence on scores of other books is evident on nearly every page of this little volume. And I owe a special word of thanks to *Eternity* magazine for allowing me to use modified material from three articles I wrote for them dealing with faith, hope, and love.

1

The Church: Myths and Meanings

A fairy tale may seem like an unusual starting point for a book about the church. But the world of *Alice in Wonderland* holds an important lesson for us.

You may recall that in the course of her wanderings, Alice came upon an egg that got larger and larger. She soon discovered that it was Humpty Dumpty. In their conversation, Humpty Dumpty used the word *glory*. And Alice said, "I don't know what you mean by *glory*."

"Of course you don't—till I tell you. . . . When I use a word," Humpty Dumpty said in a rather scornful tone, "it means just what I choose it to mean, neither more nor less."

"The question is," said Alice, "whether you can make words mean different things."

"The question is," said Humpty Dumpty, "which is to be master—that's all."

That bit of conversation is worth pondering. Humpty Dumpty was entirely right. The meanings of words do change. "The ideal of 'timeless English,' " wrote the English scholar, C. S. Lewis in one of his *Letters to Malcolm,* "is sheer nonsense. No living language can be timeless. You might as well ask for a motionless river" (Harcourt, Brace & World, 1964, p. 6). But Humpty was entirely wrong to imagine that he was master of words and could impose meanings on them according to his own whim.

What a word means today is often quite different from what it meant yesterday. But the recognition that today's meaning is different from yesterday's gives us no warrant to confuse the two, or to read today's meaning back into yesterday's word.

All this suggests that any serious study of the church should make clear today's meanings of the words as well as the New Testament meaning. That is the purpose of this first chapter.

When many people use the term *church* they have in mind a building. It has unusual features to set it off from other buildings: stained glass, or pillars out front, a steeple perhaps, but always, it seems, a mortgage. We can point to it, as we do the bank or the theater and say, "There is a church."

In the United States, religious people often use *church* to designate an organization that includes a number of congregations and buildings. It usually joins them in some program of cooperation and ministry. The church, in this sense, is a denomination, like The Evangelical Free Church of America or The Finnish Apostolic Lutheran Church of America.

Still other people use *church* to mean Christianity. These folk usually have social or cultural awareness, because they are often talking about Christian influence or ideals in society. From time to time you can hear them say, "The church must keep up the moral tone in our community," or some such statement that reveals they are thinking about influence in their town or state.

The Bible never uses the term *church* for a building, a denomination, or Christian influence in society. The term stands for something else.

And if we are to take the Bible as our standard, then there are other ideas even more dangerous than these. No one is likely to be seriously hindered in his Christian life by thinking of a building when he uses the term *church*. But other ideas can be serious threats to responsible Christian community.

The Myth of the Church as Fellowship
This is a view of the church distorted by individualism.

It says that wherever there are groups of Christians gathered in spiritual communion, there is the church. The myth gives the appearance of being the truth because it is based on a text from the Bible, a text quoted by mystics, liberals, evangelicals, and charismatics: "Where two or three are gathered together in My name, there am I in the midst of them." This is the infallible proof text for advocates of small-group Christianity.

The verse is found in Matthew 18:20, and like all texts it has a context. And like all contexts, this one is essential to understand the meaning of the text.

In the context, the Lord Jesus tells us that if our brother sins against us, we should go to him privately and seek reconciliation (v. 15). If he will not listen to us then we should take one or two others with us so that "every word may be confirmed by the evidence of two or three witnesses" (v. 16, RSV). If he refuses to listen, then Christ says, "Tell it to the church; and if he refuses to listen even to the church, let him be to you as a Gentile and a tax collector" (v. 17, RSV). The two or the three are not regarded as the church; that is identified as a larger body, locally assembled in such a way that it can be told something and the erring individual can listen to it. This particular passage makes a clear distinction between the small group of Christians and the (local) church.

Furthermore, verse 20, in the context, suggests that Jesus is in the midst of the two or three witnesses, not to have fellowship but to determine the truthfulness or falsehood of statements made in attempts to reconcile differences between believers. He is more of a judge than He is a friendly companion.

This often-quoted verse, then, does not support the idea that the essence of the church is in a few believers gathered in intimate fellowship.

The language of the Book of Acts, where we read of various small groups of Christians, is equally guarded. Take, for example, the occasion when Paul was traveling from Philippi to Troas with a substantial party consisting of Sopater, Aristarchus, Secundus, Gaius, Timothy, Tychicus, and Trophimus (Acts 20:4), together with Luke, and probably Titus. Here we have an outstanding group of Christian men who may well, on the basis of a casual (but unbiblical) definition, be regarded as "the church on the boat." But the record maintains a clear distinction between the traveling party and the churches which they visit.

Subsequently, the same party arrives at Miletus, and Paul sends to Ephesus for "the elders of the *church*," but in what follows, the church is clearly understood as back in Ephesus and not at the conference of the elders with Paul and his colleagues.

There does seem to be a biblical distinction between what properly may be described as a church and various other *ad hoc* groups of Christians, even though all of them may be true believers, and therefore, members of the church universal.

In a day when the individual often feels lost and insignificant, small groups of believers can have a vital ministry. Churches should provide members and their friends opportunities for intimate expressions of personal struggles and victories.

But that is just the point. In the New Testament, small groups served the churches; they were not the church. Cut off from the ordered life of the church, intimate little fellowships usually lapsed into unhealthy gatherings of problem-ridden individuals.

In one of his letters, C. S. Lewis' senior demon, Screwtape, instructs his junior devil, Wormwood, about the advantages of small groups in destroying the faith of a young convert and bringing him back to his evil senses. Any small group, bound together by some interest which other men dislike, he says, tends to develop into a mutual admiration hothouse. "We want the Church to be small not only that fewer men may know the Enemy but also that those who do may acquire the uneasy intensity and the defensive self-righteousness of a secret society or a clique" (C. S. Lewis, *Screwtape Letters*, Macmillan, 1951, Letter seven). I have met dozens of Christians who never recognized Satan's work in their midst.

The Myth of the Church as Invisible

This is the view of the church twisted by gnosticism. The term *gnosticism* requires some explanation. In the early days of Christianity, a group appeared that profoundly challenged the believers in biblical revelation. This group was called Gnostic because it claimed to know the secret truths of the universe (our English word *know* derives from the Greek root *gno*). And this knowledge of the Gnostic teachings was the supposed way to salvation.

Fundamental to the Gnostic system was a sharp dualism, that is, a philosophy that stressed a real, invisible world—a realm of the spirit—and a contrasting physical world, the realm of evil. Since there was no significant contact between these two realms, the system is termed *dualistic*.

We can see immediately why gnosticism challenged biblical Christianity so profoundly. Is sin a matter of ignorance? If physical bodies are evil *per se*, how could God become incarnate?

Most Christians sensed the conflict gnosticism presented to biblical truth. Their rejection was reflected in what came to be called The Apostles' Creed, which begins, "I believe in God the Father Almighty, Creator of heaven and earth. . . ." Orthodox Christians insisted that the Bible taught that physical nature and human history were spheres of genuine divine activity. The Bible states that God enters time and space and acts for our salvation.

All of this is necessary background for detecting the error of those who look for a true church beyond time and space. When a person says, "I don't belong to any church. I'm a member of the body of Christ," he is making membership in Christ a private, mystical matter, a relationship secured apart from any earthly practice, institution, or ceremony.

Such a person has the great advantage of assuming no responsibility for the organized churches on earth. All sin and failure in the churches can be dismissed as the thing that unspiritual human nature does, but it leaves the soul of the true believer untouched—and unconcerned.

The demonic element in this line of thinking is clear in Screwtape's correspondence with Wormwood. In his third letter, he tells Wormwood to keep the convert's mind off the most elementary duties by directing it to the most advanced and spiritual ones. "Aggravate that most useful human characteristic, the horror and neglect of the obvious." If you cannot keep the young man from praying for his mother, Screwtape advises, make sure "that he is always concerned with the state of her soul and never with her rheumatism . . . I have had patients of my own so well in hand that they could be turned at a moment's notice from impassioned prayer for a wife's or son's 'soul' to beating or insulting the real wife or son without a qualm" (C. S. Lewis, *Screwtape Letters,* Macmillan, 1951, Letter three).

This superspirituality has the disadvantage, however, of being foreign to the New Testament churches, which were taught that such earthly things as generous gifts of money were "graces" and a cup of water given to a thirsty brother could be given, in fact, to the Lord (Matt. 25:34-40).

The New Testament churches were recipients of invisible power and invisible companionship but the churches themselves were as earthly as tears, and blood, and fatigue.

The Myth of the Church as Original

This is the view of the church distorted by primitivism. This myth is found among those who constantly appeal to "the New Testament church"—as though the first century knew only one church, and that it was the ideal for all ages. This is a form of Christian primitivism. It looks to the original as the model. All subsequent churches are by definition poor copies, much as prints of a Rembrandt are inferior copies of the original.

The myth counterfeits an important evangelical conviction—the unique revelation of Scripture. The Word of God is the norm for all Christian teaching and behavior. *Sola Scriptura!*

But this important Reformation principle refers to the truth of God found in the Bible. It was never a blanket approval of all actions of men—Christian or non-Christian—recorded in Scripture.

Apostolic churches—think of Corinth—were often far from models. Division, heresy, immorality, and immaturity were frequently more visible than the grace of God.

The unfortunate product of this myth of the original is criticism of the churches of our time. Faultfinding is almost inevitable since it is impossible for today's churches to measure up to a model church that never existed.

The Myth of the Church as Doctrinal

This view of the church is blurred by intellectualism. It is a distortion found among those Christians who insist endlessly upon correct doctrine or "rightly dividing the Word of truth" and who feel in their hearts that without a "one hundred per cent pure" Gospel there is no true church.

Lesslie Newbigin, Bishop in Madras, India, traces this "over-intellectualizing" of faith back to the Protestant Reformers and their insistence on defining the church in terms of "rightly preached" doctrine. "The Word," said Luther, "is the one perpetual and infallible mark of the Church." Anyone, however, who has read the writings of the transformed monk will know that the Word to him meant more than correctly formulated doctrine. The Word that created faith, he believed, was dynamic and active in the souls of believers.

Nevertheless, doctrinal agreement soon became the basis of Protestant unity against the errors of Rome, and faith came to be defined in terms of agreement with church doctrine.

Many other evangelicals in the United States have a heritage of conflict with liberalism. Their view of the church is shaped by the past and they tend to think of the church in terms of "deep truths" from the Scriptures. Their church services are often classrooms in which the Bible is studied with notebook and pen in hand. A blessing, in this setting, usually means the discovery of some new idea from Scripture. And since the experience is primarily a matter of thinking, cassette tapes of the teacher's message can be distributed to hundreds of other Christians beyond the walls of the auditorium.

How many times Christian churches have been shattered by individuals or cliques who have tried to impose their myths on the body! How many zealous believers have been overwhelmed by disillusionment when they failed to find their wished-for dream in a community of Christians!

God will not allow even these tragedies to be the final word. "Only that fellowship which faces such disillusionment," says German theologian Dietrich Bonhoeffer, "with all its unhappy and ugly aspects, begins to be what it should be in God's sight, begins to grasp in faith the promise that is given to it" (*Life Together,* New York: Harper and Row, 1954, p. 27).

Before we find the church as God designed it, we must surrender the myths of our own imagination. That is why it is necessary to identify our misconceptions of the church—so that we may see more clearly the reality God offers every true believer in Jesus Christ.

What Is the Reality?

Before we discuss the form and functions of the church, we should identify it.

Perhaps the place to start is with the recognition that the church is a society of human beings, a visible community among other human communities. It has boundaries.

Theologians are usually concerned about those who have died in the faith, about "the church victorious," if you please, but the New Testament seldom—perhaps never—looks to heaven for the church. It seems satisfied to leave the dead in God's hands.

The consuming interest of the Bible is the people of God on earth. Certainly, that is the course of Christian responsibility. We are urged to join and to advance God's visible community on this planet.

As we will see in the next chapter, the heart of biblical history is the call and care of this visible community, first in Israel and then in the Christian church. In a very real sense, the 66 books of Scripture form one book, the Bible, because throughout its pages there is an actual, visible, earthly company called "the people of God."

Our Lord Jesus Christ is the "Superstar" of Scripture because, as Lesslie Newbigin has pointed out, He left behind not a book, nor a creed, nor a system of thought, nor a rule of life but a visible community—the church.

This community is special precisely because of Jesus Christ. The phrase "church of God" (*ekklesia theou*) or "church of Christ" (*ekklesia Christou*) reveals the essential meaning of the church. The word church (*ekklesia*) alone means no more than the English word "gathering." But the "church of God" indicates that this assembly's character is not in its membership but in its Head. It is God's gathering.

The New Testament teaches that all those who are brought by faith into a new relationship with Christ find themselves thereby brought into a new relationship with a host of others. The sense of being Christ's brings with it, immediately and inseparably, a sense of oneness with all Christ's people. On the broad scale, this is a *confessional* community, since it is based on a common confession, made by lip and life, that Jesus is Lord.

On a narrower scale, it is a *local* community, since the believer finds himself actually meeting together with those living in his vicinity who profess this same faith-loyalty to Jesus Christ. So when New Testament writers speak of the church (*ekklesia*), they always do so in one or the other of these two senses. And frequently we can't separate sharply the two senses.

E. Glenn Hinson, a Southern Baptist Seminary professor, suggests that the relationship between the universal and the local church is like viewing an object through two ends of a telescope. From the eyepiece, the object is greatly magnified. From the lens end, it is greatly reduced. In all respects except size, we have the same entity (*The Church: Design for Survival,* Nashville: Broadman, 1967, p. 55). The New Testament never speaks of the universal church as the sum total of all local churches. It is a totality of redeemed people, not an organization of local congregations.

Furthermore, the New Testament never suggests a conflict between the universal confessional community and the local gathered community. The New Testament writers thought of only one church because there is only one Saviour and Lord of the church. Paul underscored this unity in Ephesians 4 when he wrote, "There is one body and one Spirit—just as you were called to one hope when you were called—one Lord, one faith, one baptism, one God and Father of all, who is over all and through all and in all" (Eph. 4:4-5, NIV).

2

The Church as the People of God

Most of us recall how we chose sides for some game during childhood. Softball usually called for tossing the bat to a captain who would catch it with one hand. Then the other captain would grab the bat just above the first captain's fist. They would work their way up the handle until they reached the top. The last grip meant the first choice for team members.

Looking back over the years, I have thought more than once how cruel we used to be to the last little guy chosen. Sometimes we just tossed him on one side or the other as a token of generosity and bravado. We never considered what it felt like to be chosen last, or worse, not at all. He never complained, because who wants to be left out completely?

That memory came suddenly to mind not long ago as I read Peter's words: "Once you were not a people, but now you are the people of God; once you had not received mercy, but now you have received mercy" (1 Peter 2:10, NIV). One of the beautiful things about belonging to the church is the recognition that you are chosen. You are not left out; you are in.

There are two distinctive ways to look at the church. We can see it as part of God's plan running throughout the Bible, from Genesis to Revelation. This is the view from biblical history. Another way is to see it as a result of Christ's saving work at

Calvary and in the believer's heart. This is the view from personal salvation. In this chapter we want to see it in the first sense. In the next chapter we will see it in the second sense. Both are suggested by this text from Peter.

"You are the people of God." What did Peter mean by that? Well, obviously from the verse itself, he meant that all who have received the mercy of God in salvation, all who have renounced their moral achievements and, like the publican, prayed, "God have mercy on me, a sinner" (Luke 18:13, NIV)—are "the people of God." This is the personal view of salvation and the church.

But does Peter mean more than this? Is he suggesting some relation between the church and Israel of Old Testament times?

Christians have often struggled with the questions surrounding this relationship. Is the church the fulfillment of God's plan for Israel? Or is the church a second and alternative people of God? Is God's only design to bring individual Jews into the church today, as the fulfillment of promises made to ancient Israel, or does He retain a future purpose for corporate Israel?

These are important questions for the serious student of the Bible. They deserve our dedicated study. But for the purposes of this book, it is enough to say that the concept—*the people of God*—when applied to the church, can only be understood in the light of God's dealings with Old Testament Israel and especially His aims in the first appearance of Jesus of Nazareth.

Like some symphonic melody, references to the people of God run through those awe-inspiring events marking the birth of Jesus.

When the angel told Joseph that the Holy Spirit was responsible for Mary's pregnancy, he commanded Joseph to name the baby *Jesus*—the Greek version of the Old Testament *Joshua* meaning "the Lord is Saviour." That name had special significance, the angel explained, because Jesus would "save *His people* from their sins" (Matt. 1:21, RSV).

Thus, the name *Jesus*, so dear to Christians, provided a link between God's people in the Old Testament and God's people in the New. The Baby in Bethlehem's stall was both the fulfillment of God's promise to Israel and the foundation of God's plan for the church.

Both ideas appear in the nativity events. Elizabeth's husband Zacharias, when filled with the Spirit, prophesied of the unborn Jesus: "Praise the Lord, the God of Israel because He has come and has redeemed *His people.*" The old priest seemed to be speaking of Israel. A bit later, however, another elder in Israel, Simeon, saw in the Baby "salvation . . . prepared in the sight of *all people,* a light for revelation to the Gentiles and for glory to Your people Israel" (Luke 1:68 and 2:30-32, NIV). Simeon's vision carried him forward to the new people of God, the church.

Clearly, then, the life of Jesus marks a significant turning point in the unfolding drama of the people of God in Scripture. In Him, the promises to Abraham, Moses, and David find fulfillment and a new people of God is created. We can learn a lot about the church by studying the basic ideas surrounding the concept of the people of God. Three of these basic ideas will be explored in this chapter.

A Called People

We learn, first, that the church is a community of people—the people of God—who owe their existence and their distinctiveness to one fundamental fact—the call of God.

The call came first to Abraham. God told him to leave his country and kindred and to go to another country where God would make of him another people. Abraham's tribe would be God's means of enriching all people on the earth (Gen. 12:1-3).

Several times God confirmed this covenant of grace—this spiritual agreement—with Abraham (Gen. 22:17-18). Later, it was confirmed to Abraham's son, Isaac, and to Isaac's son Jacob. But Jacob died in Egyptian captivity, as did his distinguished son Joseph. This series of setbacks explains that prosaic note which closes the Book of Genesis. Joseph died, he was embalmed and "put in a coffin in Egypt" (Gen. 50:26, RSV).

God's promise, however, moved rapidly toward fulfillment under Moses, who descended from Jacob's son Levi. Moses led the despised slaves out of Egypt by a miraculous exodus and three months after their deliverance from the Pharaoh, they entered the wilderness of Sinai. Here the Lord told Moses to say to the people:

"You have seen . . . how I bore you on eagles' wings and brought you to Myself. Now therefore, if you will obey My voice and keep My covenant, you shall be My own possession among all peoples, for all the earth is Mine and you shall be to Me a kingdom of priests and a holy nation" (Ex. 19:4-6, RSV).

"You shall be My people," said the Lord, *"if you obey My voice."* Israel, then, was created and sustained by the voice of God, the word that came to them in the wilderness.

God wanted His people to know that their uniqueness among the tribes of the desert and the nations of the Near East rested on their hearing and obeying His Word. They did not choose to follow God; God chose to call them. Their obedience to the Law given at Sinai was never a means of securing God's favor. There is no hint that God loved them because they were good. Their obedience was the way of life appropriate for a delivered people.

Later, by God's outstretched arm they conquered Canaan and later still they established a monarchy. Unfortunately, it ended in disaster. God's people broke His covenant, rejected His Law and despised His prophets, until there was no remedy. The judgment of God fell upon them, and the Babylonian captivity began.

Yet God did not abandon His people. In time, true to His promise to bless them, He called them out of Babylon, as He had called them out of Egypt, and He restored them to their land. As God said through Jeremiah: "Therefore, behold, the days are coming, says the Lord, when it shall no longer be said, 'As the Lord lives who brought up the people of Israel out of the land of Egypt,' but 'As the Lord lives who brought up the people of Israel out of the north country and out of all the countries where He had driven them.' For I will bring them back to their own land which I gave to their fathers" (Jer. 16:14-15, RSV).

But God also promised through His people to bless all the nations of the earth. Israel's disobedience made this impossible until "the fulness of times" and the coming of Christ. For God's call into the land of Canaan, first of Abraham's family from Ur and Haran, then of Jacob's descendants from Egypt, and of the remnant of Judah from Babylon, all foreshadowed a better call and a greater redemption. Through the death and resurrection of

Jesus, God's purpose is to call out of the world a people for Himself, to redeem them from sin, and to give them His promised salvation.

This call is the heart of the New Testament understanding of the church. The idea is cradled in the term most often used to designate the church. The Greek term *ekklesia* is built upon the root of the verb *kaleō* meaning "to call." The *ekklesia,* then, is the assembly or congregation called together.

The church, therefore, is more than an aggregation—people who choose to come together. It is a congregation—people who have been called together by the Word of God. In that sense, God is first. His call precedes the assembly. The body gathers, not to share their thoughts and opinions, but to listen to the voice of God.

The New Testament insists strongly upon this fact. God has called us "into the fellowship of His Son" (1 Cor. 1:9, RSV), called us, in fact, "to belong to Jesus Christ" (Rom. 1:6, RSV). This divine call is "a holy calling" (2 Tim. 1:9, RSV) or a calling "in holiness" (1 Thes. 4:7, RSV) which separates us from the world and makes us in character and conduct "saints" (1 Cor. 1:2, RSV).

Three practical lessons emerge from this special calling of the people of God. First, if the church is called by God, it must assemble. God's Word is an invitation to the guilty and the lonely to leave the world and to find not only forgiveness but also community in Him. He calls us from our isolation to be joined to a people, assembled for praise and care and mission. This is the primary biblical reason for corporate worship. We do not attend church to be entertained. We go to church to give visible and audible expression to what we are, members of a unique body, distinct from the world, the people of God.

Second, if the church is called by the Word of God, then the Bible should have a central place in the gatherings of His people. We learn about our need of salvation, and feel the sting of a convicted conscience, and discover God's way of holiness through the preaching and teaching of Scripture.

Third, the call of God should destroy our spiritual complacency. Saints never fully achieve; they never arrive. The church is always a pilgrim people on the way. Paul's attitude is our model here: "Not that I have already obtained . . . or have already been made perfect, but I press on to take hold of that for which Christ Jesus took hold of me" (Phil. 3:12, NIV). God always calls His people to greater Christlikeness and selfless service because "the prize of the high calling of God" is Jesus Christ, nothing less.

A Covenant People

The church is also a community of people—the people of God—who are bound to one another because they are bound to God—in a covenant.

Covenants were common ways that people entered into agreements in the ancient world. A covenant bound friend to friend (1 Sam. 18:3), or established water rights between two tribal leaders (Gen. 21:22-32), or expressed the terms of peace between two kings (1 Kings 20:34). Naturally, then, a covenant came to express the relation between God and Israel (and later the church).

Long ago, our fathers in the faith recognized the central place of the covenant in biblical history when they distinguished Old Covenant from New Covenant or, as we came to call them, Old Testament and New Testament.

The titles indicate that the underlying reality that binds the Bible together is the covenant. It is not the covenant idea, however, that unites the Scriptures. It is the covenant itself, an action taken by God in history, which results in a binding relationship between the Lord and His people. The Old Covenant, created by the Exodus and Sinai, sustained Israel. The New Covenant, created by the death and resurrection of Jesus, sustains the church.

This central place of the covenant compels us to examine the nature of the covenant and its significance first for Israel, then for the church.

The first element of the covenant was its personal character. The covenant involved special acts of a personal God with a nation of persons. It was not the discovery of certain spiritual laws by the ancient Jews. Nor was it the creation of a set of religious ideas by some men of outstanding religious genius. It was rather the willing response of people entering into a unique relationship with God at a decisive moment in their history. It was probably the most important event in Israel's life story.

God said to Israel at Sinai, "I bore you on eagles' wings and brought you to Myself" (Ex. 19:4, RSV). That is the heart of covenant. Ideas and laws do not speak. They cannot *draw us*. Only a living Person can do that!

In the church, the personal character of the covenant is retained by the personal faith of the members in the death and resurrection of Jesus. There is no Christianity by proxy. Each of us must surrender to the Lord personally—because we recognize our slavery to sin and our need of redemption.

A little girl once splashed through a puddle and got mud on her socks. After examining it with a critical eye she asked her mother, "What's mud for?" Her mother searched rapidly for a convincing answer, and found it. "For making bricks, dear."

"What are bricks for?"

"Making houses, dear."

"What are houses for?"

"People."

The little girl paused only for a second and then asked the question to which her mother had no reply.

"And what are people for?"

The basic idea behind the covenant with God holds the answer to that question. The covenant, first with Israel, then with the church, says, "These people are for God!"

The second element in the covenant was its origin. It was established by God, then received by men. It was not an agreement between equals, a bargain which man struck with the Almighty. Pagan religions surrounding Israel were filled with such ideas of covenant. Their devotees were desperately trying to somehow please the gods in order to enter into an agreement and escape their wrath. In striking contrast to this, Israel's covenant was not one they offered to God. It was rather one He offered to them. God took the initiative, and presented the covenant to them. He chose them to be His people before they chose Him to be their God.

The third aspect of the covenant was its basis. It was grounded in God's mercy, not in the worthiness or the achievement of man. Israel could never claim that, because of their number or power or goodness or cleverness, they were called to be God's people. On the contrary, they were the unworthy objects of God's unbelievable love. They were the recipients of amazing grace. "It was not because you were more in number than any other people that the Lord set His love upon you and chose you, for you were the fewest of all peoples; but it is because the Lord loves you" (Deut. 7:7-8, RSV).

Here was something absolutely unheard-of in history. Other gods terrorized their worshipers and men feverishly attempted to bribe their gods by sacrificial offerings. But in Israel a loving God stepped into history, broke the bonds of Egypt's cruelty and made a people of no people.

When the church senses that God has done the same for her, she lifts her voice and sings with the hymnwriter, Samuel Davies:

O may this strange, this matchless grace,
This Godlike miracle of love
Fill the whole earth with grateful praise,
And all th' angelic choirs above.
Who is a pard'ning God like Thee?
Or who has grace so rich and free?

Some students of the Bible have overlooked this note of grace in the Old Covenant. In their desire to magnify the grace of God in the Gospel, they have argued that Israel entered into a legal relationship with God at Sinai. Somehow, Israel was supposed to earn God's favor by keeping the Law.

But that is to accept the Pharisee's view of the Law as God's view. The relationship of the Old Covenant was not based on achievement or reward. It was secured by God's power and mercy, displayed in the exodus from slavery. The Law did not establish Israel's relation to God; the Law elaborated the lifestyle of God's redeemed people.

Scribes and Pharisees would in time see the Law and all its surrounding traditions as a means of gaining God's approval. But at Sinai God's intent seemed clear. He delivered His people from bondage; then, He gave them the Law. The order is important.

Exodus 20:1-3 says, "God spoke. . . . I am the Lord thy God, which brought thee out of the land of Egypt. . . . Thou shalt have no other gods before Me."

Unfortunately, Israel's later history was marked by deepening disobedience to God. The prophets reminded and rebuked the people of God but, in Hosea's words, their hearts were set on other lovers (Hosea 2:7). They loved their sin.

Finally, Jeremiah saw no hope except in a new covenant: "But this is the covenant which I will make with the house of Israel . . . says the Lord: 'I will put My law within them, and I will write it upon their hearts; and I will be their God, and they shall be My people'" (Jer. 31:33, RSV). People like Joseph and Mary, and Simeon and Anna lived in the light of this hope until God chose to send His Son, "the guarantee" of this "better covenant" (Heb. 7:22, NIV).

No doubt, early Christians saw themselves as heirs of this tradition in Israel. They were the faithful remnant which looked not at their own religious purity but to the grace of God as their hope of salvation. Certainly, Jeremiah's promise is behind the early Christian understanding of the Lord's Supper as "the New Covenant" (2 Cor. 11:25; Matt. 26:28). The death of Christ, symbolized in the cup of the communion meal, is the basis of a new relationship with God. This relationship is also expressed by God's Law—but the Law is no longer written on tablets of stone. It is engraved on the hearts of God's new people, the church of Jesus Christ.

A Chosen People

Finally, we learn that the church is a community of people—the people of God—who are chosen by God to reflect the glory of God and to spread the Gospel to all people.

That, I take it, is the heart of the biblical doctrine of election. The word *election* scares many people speechless. It conjures up images of somber Calvinists and black-caped Puritans. Didn't Jonathan Edwards, who preached "Sinners in the Hands of an Angry God," believe in election? Who wants to return to that?

Such fears are not without foundation. The doctrine of election in the hands of some Christians has been distorted beyond biblical recognition. The Calvinistic tradition, in particular, starting from a justifiable desire to eliminate all thoughts of man earning salvation, stressed the sovereign freedom of God to choose and regenerate whomever He wills. It has often defended election, however, as an arbitrary decree of God settled in eternity. In this way of thinking, the true church easily becomes a mysterious company of the invisible elect known only to God.

The result of this thinking is often the removal of the actual church on earth from the central place it holds in the New Testament records and especially the displacement of the missionary task from the heart of Christian concern and obedience.

Under the influence of Captain Cook's adventures in the South Sea Islands, and the teaching of his friend, Andrew Fuller, William Carey began preaching the worldwide obligations of the Gospel. At one ministers' meeting he proposed the preachers discuss the necessity of carrying the Good News to those who had never heard. Old John Ryland grew angry with him for meddling in God's affairs. "Sit down, young man," he said. "When God wills to convert the heathen, He'll do it without your help or mine."

That is a doctrine of election without New Testament support, built upon philosophical conclusions rather than biblical revelation.

In the New Testament, election is rooted in historic fact, especially in Jesus Christ who was crucified under Pontius Pilate. He is the elect One of God, the Father's beloved Son (Matt. 3:17). Our election is only by our union with Him. We are not chosen as isolated individuals, but as members of His body, the church.

The instrument of God's choosing in the Bible is the preaching of the Gospel of Jesus' death and resurrection. That is how Paul saw it. He recalled his ministry to the Thessalonians and he reminded them of its result: "Brothers loved by God, we know that He has chosen you, because our Gospel came to you not simply with words, but also with power, with the Holy Spirit and with deep conviction" (1 Thes. 1:4-5, NIV).

Christian theologians have usually been concerned with the *reasons* for election or the lack of reasons. The Bible, however, offers us no reasons. It stresses the *purpose* of election. It allows the mystery of God's choosing to stand without explanation and concentrates instead on the quality of life the church is called to exhibit.

God said to Israel at Sinai: "You shall be to Me a kingdom of priests and *a holy nation*" (Ex. 19:6, RSV). And Paul wrote to the Ephesians: God chose us in Christ "before the creation of the world to be holy and blameless in His sight" (Eph. 1:4, NIV).

Nowhere in Scripture does it suggest that *elect* means "favorite." If anything, *elect* stands for "instrument" because God chose Israel to be a "kingdom of priests," that is, a people to mediate the mercies of God to those who are without mercy.

That distinction is absolutely imperative. It is one Lesslie Newbigin makes forcefully when he writes: "Wherever the missionary character of the doctrine of election is forgotten; wherever it is forgotten that we are chosen in order to be sent; . . . wherever men think that the purpose of election is their own salvation rather than the salvation of the world; then God's people have betrayed their trust" (*The Household of God,* New York: Friendship Press, 1954, p. 111).

The doctrine of election, then, far from being dated and irrelevant, is a fundamental explanation of the church's reason for existence.

If the church is the company of the elect—and it is—it has no cause to boast, because the truth of God and the grace of God are ours not to hoard but to give away. The invitation to receive the Gospel is also a mandate to share it with others. That is why the only church the Bible knows is a missionary church.

And that brings us back to our starting point because in the passage which launched this chapter—1 Peter 2:9-10—the Apostle struck this missionary note. He reminded his readers that they were "God's own people, that you may declare the wonderful deeds of Him who called you out of darkness into His marvelous light" (1 Peter 2:9, RSV). And that is a note worth sounding again and again.

3

Salvation and the Church

Back in the turbulent 60s a button appeared in California. Like hundreds of buttons during those days it had a message. It read: "Jesus, Yes! The Church, No!"

Perhaps one of the greatest barriers to men and women coming to God is the church itself. To most people, it is all too evident that the church is a human institution. It struggles with power and pride, with greed and lust, not in the hidden individual member alone, but in the highest levels of religious leadership.

"The church is like Noah's ark," one late medieval manuscript read. "If it weren't for the storm outside, you couldn't stand the smell inside."

That is stark realism! In our time many may even prefer the storm to the smell.

One basic truth was presented in the last chapter: that the salvation of a people—the people of God—a corporate body—has always been, and still is, the great purpose of God in time.

We argued that under the Old Covenant, arranged at Sinai after the exodus from Egypt, God provided for the salvation of Israel. Under the New Covenant, secured at Calvary and Joseph's tomb, God extended salvation to the church.

We tried to show that the church is crucial to God's plans in human history. In this chapter we want to argue that the church is also central to God's purposes in the human heart. If it is true that God needs a special people to witness to the world, it is equally true that a believer needs a family in which to grow.

Christianity Is Corporate

Few people in our time believe that God's purpose is to create a believing body and use it for the enrichment of persons. Even Christians have trouble with that idea.

In order to avoid the embarrassment created by the church, some believers have tried to make the real church something above the failures and sins of the people who make up the church on earth.

"Free the faith from criticism! Exempt it from time, space and sin. In a word, separate Christ from the church. Jesus, yes! The church, no!"

The most popular form of this purgation of the faith is to make Christianity strictly a private affair—and limit spiritual relationships to *ad hoc* experiences. Attend a Bible conference or a "Christian" rock concert but don't talk church membership. That way, you can have Jesus with no strings attached.

This outlook is roughly comparable to free love. When the urge to make love hits you, do it! But never discuss marriage; never think of love as responsibility.

The great difficulty with this highly individualistic view of religion is that it offers no safeguard from the deceitfulness of the individual *psyche* (Jer. 17:9). If I retreat to my private soul, who will free me from myself? How will I distinguish the voice of God from the voice of pride?

Fortunately, most Christians do not go so far as to reject the church entirely. They are still handicapped, however, by an individualistic view of salvation that sees the church only in terms of personal advantage.

Sometimes, the attitude comes out in our advice to new Christians. We tell a young convert that in order to grow in his faith, he ought to read his Bible and pray every day. And since he needs fellowship, he ought to go to church.

But isn't that a shallow reason for going to church? Haven't we already planted the seed of destruction for any true worship—what do I get out of it?

If we pursue our love-marriage analogy, let's apply the same line of argument to a wedding. Can you imagine telling a young bridegroom, "I'm glad you are getting married; you will get so much out of it"? Weddings are not for those looking to receive; they are for those prepared to give themselves away.

And what happens if the church fails to provide fellowship for our young convert? What if he happens to enjoy a religious commune more than the church?

Young believers need to see that the church is part and parcel of true salvation, just as marriage is inextricably linked to true love. To love truly, one assumes responsibility for the loved one. That is marriage. To be saved truly, one is added to a body of saved ones. That is the church.

I do not want to be misunderstood. I am not denying the point I made in the last chapter about the covenant establishing a relationship between *persons*. After all, what could be more personal than the evangelical experience of the saved soul? Surely that personal note is an authentic theme within biblical religion.

The burdened and needy sinner cannot come to God by proxy. We do not sing: "When *we* survey the wondrous cross." It is "*my* richest gain" that is counted loss. It is I who must come to the mercy seat, alone.

But while saving faith is an intensely personal matter, it is never a purely private matter.

Man, as God has made him, is an individual ego, but not an isolated ego. According to the Bible, self-centered isolation is the corruption of human nature; it is the supreme illustration, not of grace, but of sin.

This is precisely the purpose of redemption: to free us from our self-centeredness. Christ died on the cross and the Spirit came at Pentecost to dethrone the sinful self and draw us into a new community. In the New Testament, the Christian life is not accidentally, but necessarily, corporate. If a member of the body should say, "I do not belong to the body," it would not for that reason cease to be part of the body (1 Cor. 12:15, NIV).

Sin in the Church

If God's will for Christian believers is life in some corporate fellowship, how shall charges against the church be answered? How shall sin in the church be explained?

Christians have often felt the sting of this indictment. Roman Catholic theologians, for example, have frequently argued that since the church is the body of Christ, it cannot sin. Her members sin, but the church as such is free from sin. And in the sacrament of penance the church has the means of dealing with the sins of her members.

This line of argument, however, really evades the problem. Which honest person can deny that the church as a visible society has often been guilty of pride, unbelief, and greed? The neat distinction between the church and her members is an abstraction. Luther recognized this when he said, "The face of the church is the face of the sinner."

The New Testament clearly teaches that the church sins. To the same church—at Corinth—Paul wrote, "Ye are the body of Christ" (1 Cor. 12:27) and "Ye are yet carnal" (1 Cor. 3:3).

Furthermore, the New Testament suggests that a church can sin so grievously and so frequently that it can be in danger of death. The Lord of the church said to the church at Sardis, "You have a reputation for being alive, but you are dead" (Rev. 3:1, NIV). And he warned the Ephesians, "If you do not repent, I will come to you and remove your lampstand from its place" (Rev. 2:5, NIV).

The use of the term *church,* therefore, is not enough. A church can disobey God and sin against the Holy Spirit to the point of transgressing the line of church existence. It can become a non-church. We have no reason, then, to deny that the church has sinned and does sin.

But to look for a sinless church is to miss the whole point of the church's existence. The church is a community between the times—between the first and second coming of Jesus. Life in Christ is both a gift of God already accepted and a reality not yet complete. The new life of the Spirit is a kind of down payment for our full inheritance yet to come (Eph. 1:13-14).

So the church lives by hope. It knows that in this present age it can never claim final victory over sin. That has to await the return of the Victor.

Until then, the church is under the Cross. God's grace and God's power come only through death. And that is why our witness is never about the merit of the church but about the grace and power of Christ:

Nothing in my hand I bring
Simply to Thy cross I cling.

We sing this in church because we no longer think of the church as a perfect society. In one sense the church—as Puritan Richard Baxter once said—is "a mere hospital." How long has it been since you heard someone castigate the hospital as worthless because its patients were sick?

So let's agree that God's will for the Christian is life in the fellowship of the church and that this community of believers, this side of Christ's return, is always in need of God's grace because it is marred by sin.

The Portrait of the Church

If church fellowship is always a smudged likeness of God's ultimate plan for His people, what can we reasonably expect from a congregation of believers?

In describing the character of the Christian community, the New Testament usually resorts to figures of speech. We call them metaphors. In examining these images, we need to recognize that they are both descriptive and prescriptive. They describe what the church is as God designed it. And they prescribe what the church ought to become as Christ shapes its experience in a given place during a particular time.

Jesus, quite naturally, spoke of His followers in terms He borrowed from the Old Testament. Three of the most picturesque are bride, vineyard, and flock. Any Jew, of course, would think of the Lord of Israel choosing His bride, planting His vineyard, and shepherding His flock.

Isaiah had written, "As the bridegroom rejoices over the bride, so shall your God rejoice over you" (Isa. 62:5, RSV). Jesus adopted this imagery to explain why fasting was inappropriate for

His disciples. He, the bridegroom, was still with His wedding guests (the disciples) so they had every reason to be happy. The day would come, however, when the bridegroom would be taken away from them; then they would fast (Mark 2:18-20).

The vineyard image also comes from Isaiah. "My beloved had a vineyard on a very fertile hill," the prophet sang. "He digged it and cleared it of stones, and planted it with choice vines . . . and he looked for it to yield grapes, but it yielded wild grapes" (Isa. 5:1-2, RSV).

Jesus used this image in His parable of the wicked husbandmen, who beat the servants of the vineyard Owner and killed His Son (Mark 12:1-11). But Jesus also extended the picture. In another context, He claimed to be the Vine itself, whose branches could bear fruit only by abiding in Him (John 15:1-11).

The flock idea, like the other two, can be found in Isaiah. In the passage immortalized by Handel's *Messiah,* the prophet predicted: He will feed His flock like a shepherd, He will gather the lambs in His arms, He will carry them in His bosom, and gently lead those that are with young (Isa. 40:11, RSV).

In the teaching of Jesus, He is the Good Shepherd venturing into the wilderness to search for a single, lost lamb (Luke 15:3-7). He leads His sheep into pleasant pastures and finally lays down His life for His sheep (John 10:1-18).

From these three metaphors, we can conclude that Jesus' followers are (1) joined to Him by a spiritual covenant, (2) intended to be fruitful, that is, pleasing to the Lord, and (3) protected and nourished by Jesus Himself because He loves them, even unto death.

The Apostle Paul used three other figures for additional insight into the church: the body, the family, and the building.

The Body of Christ

Paul's favorite figure for the church was the *body,* the only New Testament metaphor without some Old Testament background. The Apostle used it in Ephesians, Colossians, Romans, and 1 Corinthians.

What does the term mean? Many American evangelical

Christians understand it to mean no more than the body of Christians, that is, a collection of individual believers. The term certainly may include all who are in Christ, but the Bible does not say "the body of Christians." It says "the body of Christ."

Another possibility is "the community which belongs to Christ." This view takes "of Christ" as a possessive and therefore sets the church off from all other bodies.

Finally, *body of Christ* may mean "the organism which is united with Christ." The body is more than a mere collection of individuals. It is a spiritual organism. Believers in Christ are united in His body because they are, through regeneration, united with the Head.

This third understanding is likely the meaning that Paul intended. While it is true that the church belongs to Christ—He "purchased" it with His blood (Acts 20:28)—the union of Christ with His people and their unity with each other is Paul's basic meaning.

In Ephesians and Colossians, the Apostle seemed to view the body in its widest possible dimensions because he saw it joined to its exalted Head. Paul stated in Ephesians 1:22-23 that God has "put all things under His [Jesus'] feet and has made Him the Head over all things for the church which is His body, the fulness of Him who fills all in all" (RSV).

The Apostle seemed to suggest that the exaltation of Christ has cosmic significance. Certainly, it is a view of the church that reaches beyond the local congregation—without, of course, denying the church as a congregation.

In Romans and 1 Corinthians, however, the local assembly of believers was in Paul's mind. And his primary point in using the body imagery was to stress the diversity of the members within the unity of the body, the church. Romans 12:4-5 summarizes the idea best: "Just as each of us has one body with many members, and these members do not all have the same function, so in Christ we who are many form one body, and each member belongs to all the others" (NIV).

The essential character of the church, we should notice, is not the result of several members agreeing to constitute a body. The members represent the diversity, not the unity. The unity of the body arises from Christ alone.

In spite of the widespread acceptance of the idea in the United States, the church is not a voluntary association. Members are not added, nor are they separated by personal choice. If they belong to Christ, then they belong to each other since He, not they, constitutes the oneness. As Paul stated in Romans, we form one body *in Christ*.

If Christians ever came to see that truth, it would make them more tolerant of brothers and sisters in the church with whom they have differences. Diversity is not something to be rejected; it is something to be embraced. God intends it as a means of ministering to the body, and through the body to the world. Every member, therefore, is important in the eyes of God.

The Family of God

The second figure Paul used to describe the church is *family*. This suggests that the church is a fellowship of love and acceptance.

The idea is implicit in the thought, often used by Jesus, that God is our Father. But Paul, in Ephesians 2:19, stated plainly that we are no longer foreigners and aliens but "members of God's household" (NIV).

That would indicate that becoming a Christian is like getting married. You fall in love, you commit yourself to another, you become one in interests and desires; and you acquire in-laws. The Bible simply doesn't recognize a Christianity of the rugged individual.

In his *Journal*, John Wesley, the founder of Methodism, mentions the advice given to him by an unnamed "serious man." "Sir," the man said, "you wish to serve God and go to heaven? Remember that you cannot serve Him alone. You must therefore find companions, or make them; the Bible knows nothing of solitary religion."

American evangelicals have an exciting heritage in the history of revivalism. This movement of mass evangelism aimed at the conversion of individuals made its mark on the American character. It tamed a wilderness and shaped public morality for a century after the War of Independence.

Revivalism, however, created the impression that a decision for Christ was the beginning and end of Christian experience. All else was secondary, if not worthless. Many believers still believe that getting saved is about all there is to being a Christian.

No one should challenge the crucial importance of a personal conversion. Jesus Himself told Nicodemus, "Unless a man is born again, he cannot see the kingdom of God" (John 3:3, NIV). But the new birth implies a family. How can we have God as our Father without at the same time accepting God's children as our brothers and sisters?

The church is God's way of meeting a deep-seated need in the human heart, the need to belong. The writer of Genesis put it profoundly but simply when he recorded God's creation of man. Creative day after creative day God had looked at His handiwork and pronounced it good—the stars, the cattle, the shrubs, the shrimp. But when He came to man, He said, "It isn't good for man to be alone" (Gen. 2:18, LB).

The hosts of human clubs, societies, lodges, and fraternities testify to man's social need—the Pessimists' Club, the Royal Society of Muskrats, the Cosmic Community of the Twice Born. The list is endless. "Joinitis" is a human affliction because God has made us with a hunger for fellowship.

What is the most excruciating punishment in our penal institutions? Solitary confinement. Why? Because loneliness is hell. God created us for communion, and the marred image of God in man still witnesses to this thirst that cannot be quenched.

The church, however, as God designed it, is a foretaste of the delights of a city with foundations, a holy city, in which God will dwell with His people (Rev. 21:2-4).

The Temple of the Spirit

The third figure Paul used to describe the church was the *building,* or more particularly "the temple." The image appears in the First Letter to the Corinthians (3:10-17) and in the Ephesian correspondence (2:20-22). In both passages we find three truths about the church:

First, the church has a changeless foundation. Its character for all time is determined by its cornerstone, Jesus Christ, and by the revelation God gave, once for all, through inspired apostles and prophets (1 Cor. 3:10; Eph. 2:20). Man may build on that foundation—the Gospel of our Lord Jesus Christ—but no man can remove it or lay another one.

Second, the building, the church, is still under construction. It is not complete. It must always be accepted for what it is in its incomplete state. God insists that we learn to live with approximations of the fulness of the building. That is the life of faith.

But that is precisely what some people reject. As we have seen, there are those who want a church "without spot or wrinkle" now. But that attitude misses a very important point: the church, like the individual believer, can only be understood in grace. The church is not for those who have arrived; it is composed of pilgrims, who are on the way.

Third, the temple, the church, is the dwelling place of God. He fills it with His presence and glory.

Most of us have never been in a temple, so it is hard for us to recapture the attitudes and emotions the Jews felt in their holy place. One biblical passage, however, reveals the reverence one man experienced.

"In the year that King Uzziah died," Isaiah wrote, "I saw the Lord sitting upon a throne, high and lifted up; and His train [afterglow] filled the temple" (Isa. 6:1, RSV).

If the church is the temple of God, our congregations, above all else, ought to be places where men see God. Are we in any way blurring the vision of God? When men and women lose their "King Uzziahs" can they find God in our churches?

Isaiah also heard a voice calling, "Holy, holy, holy is the Lord of hosts; the whole earth is full of His glory." And the prophet cried, "Woe is me! For I am a man of unclean lips" (Isa. 6:3-5, RSV).

When Isaiah witnessed the glory of God in the temple, he saw his own sin. Shouldn't the church also reflect the glory of

God in such a way that men see their sin and cry "Woe is me"? I am sure that is what the Apostle intended when he called the church "the temple of God."

The Corinthian congregation, we know, was rent with rival parties, each following some Christian leader. They had lost the sense of unity in Christ and were in danger of destroying the church. To these factious Corinthians, Paul wrote: "Don't you know that you yourselves are God's temple and that God's Spirit lives in you? If anyone destroys God's temple, God will destroy him; for God's temple is sacred, and you are that temple" (1 Cor. 3:16-17, NIV). When we recognize that God is in His temple, indwelling His church, we will often be driven to our knees in confession of our sin.

Isaiah discovered one last thing in the temple. One of the seraphim took a burning coal from the altar and touched the prophet's lips. "Your guilt is taken away," he said.

Then Isaiah heard the voice of the Lord saying, "Whom shall I send, and who will go for Us?" The prophet responded, "Here am I! Send me."

Isaiah saw the Lord, recognized his sin, and then discovered God's purpose for his life. All this in the temple of God! "Now," says the Apostle Paul, "you, the church, are the temple of God." What a vision for God's people! What a high calling for any congregation of believers!

These are the reasons the New Testament knows no "solitary religion." It understands that man's basic need is the restoration of community, fellowship with God, and reconciliation with others. That is why full salvation always means life in the family of God, the church of Jesus Christ.

4

The Growth of the Church

In one of my favorite *Peanuts* cartoons, Lucy demands that Linus change TV channels and then threatens him with her fist if he doesn't.

"What makes you think you can walk right in here and take over?" asks Linus.

"These five fingers," says Lucy. "Individually they're nothing but when I curl them together like this into a single unit, they form a weapon that is terrible to behold."

"Which channel do you want?" asks Linus.

Turning away, he looks at his fingers and says, "Why can't you guys get organized like that?"

Mobilizing for effective action is always a problem. We find the standard for an effective church, however, in Acts 2:36-46. " 'Therefore, let all Israel be assured of this: God has made this Jesus whom you crucified both Lord and Christ.' When the people heard this, they were cut to the heart and said to Peter and the other Apostles, 'Brothers, what shall we do?' Peter replied: 'Repent and be baptized, every one of you, in the name of Jesus Christ so that your sins may be forgiven. And you will receive the gift of the Holy Spirit.' . . . Those who accepted his message were baptized, and about three thousand were added to their number that day. They devoted themselves to the Apostles' teaching and to the fellowship, to the breaking of bread and to prayer" (Acts 2:36-38, 41-42, NIV).

Here we have the church in its prime, when the memory of Jesus was fresh and the gift of the Spirit was new. Here God has given us a model of a growing church. In doing so, God has left us a timeless reminder that the church is more than an informal fellowship of saved individuals. It is a community of faith to which members are added. As the Holy Spirit convicts men of sin, and as they repent of their sin and trust in Christ for salvation, they are baptized and received into the church. That is the heart of church expansion. Four principles of church growth are clear in this passage.

Intensity of Preaching

Peter's message on the Day of Pentecost was aimed at *convincing the minds* of his listeners. He tried to persuade them that Jesus was the Messiah (Acts 2:36). He wasn't content with empty decision. He wanted their response to be rooted in reasons.

He did more than inform, however; he struck at their moral sense. He aimed at *convicting their consciences* and they were "cut to the heart" (v. 37). They saw the moral consequences of their rejection of Jesus.

Peter concluded by *communicating the hope* of the Gospel. "The promise is to you," he told them (v. 39). He offered them forgiveness for their heinous crime of putting to death the Lord of Glory, and he promised them the gift of the Spirit for the power to change. With preaching like that, no wonder this infant church grew not by twos or tens but by thousands!

From time to time, preaching, like everything else associated with the Christian church, comes under fire. Some skeptics have questioned its place in the church at all. In his *Incendiary Fellowship,* Christian educator and author, Elton Trueblood says, "I think it likely that the men who derogate preaching are, for the most part, precisely those who cannot do it well" (New York: Harper and Row, 1967, p. 48). Whether that is true or false, the rejection of preaching isn't open to a church concerned with biblical obedience because the church, as God intended it, lives and grows by the proclamation and practice of the Gospel. "Faith," said Paul, "comes from hearing the message, and the message is heard through the word of Christ" (Rom. 10:17, NIV).

Styles of preaching will change but the power of preaching never. Preaching, in the sense of bringing the Word of God to bear upon the minds and consciences of men, is the lifeblood of a growing church.

Our greatest danger is that we make preaching the province of the pros. We need professionals, but preaching in the Early Church was little more than "gossiping the Gospel." One beggar telling another beggar where to find bread. In the second century, Celsus, an outspoken critic of Christianity, complained of the Christians at work, in the laundry, in the schoolroom, at the street corner, who were always "jabbering away" about their Jesus.

In one sense, church growth is no great mystery. You can do one of two things. You either get hungry people to the Bread or you take the Bread of Life to hungry people. It is the preacher's job to bring supply and demand together.

One of the simplest tests of effective preaching I have ever heard came not from a preacher but from a playwright. Arthur Miller, the famous writer and critic, was once asked, "How can you tell a good play?" And he said, "When I am forced to sit up straight and say, 'That's me!' "

That is how Peter preached and his audience asked, "What shall we do?"

Integrity of Membership

What did this apostolic fellowship do with its converts? It is necessary to raise that question because so much evangelism in our time ends in the soul of the convert. Many decisions for Christ have no relation to membership in the church. Not so in apostolic evangelism. Acts 2:41 shows that those who responded to Peter's message did three things: (1) they accepted Peter's call to repentance, (2) they confessed their faith in Christ by baptism, and (3) they were added to the church.

Repentance is a change of heart, a moral about-face. It is agreeing with the Gospel's indictment of our crimes against heaven. It is a term we seldom hear today. We hear much about how God loves us, but not much about how we hate Him. Any Gospel which saves, however, makes men worse before it makes them better. As Vance Havner, the southern evangelist, once said, "No one can say 'Praise God,' until he has said, 'Woe is me!' " And that "woe is me" becomes a characteristic of a Christian's lifestyle.

Young couples who make a success of their marriages discover early that weddings do not survive on the basis of certificates alone. In the day-to-day friction of two egocentric personalities, they learn to say, "I was wrong and I'm sorry."

As with marriages, so with churches. There will be little growth where people refuse to say, "I'm sorry." How many conflicts, disagreements, and separations could be avoided if elders, trustees, deacons, pastors, and choir members were men and women who were willing to repent and say, "I was wrong and I'm sorry."

These converts were also *baptized*. The Apostles knew that you do not build churches on the quicksands of mere decision. Nothing is less stable than the good intentions of the human heart! That is why we need institutions.

Peter told these converts that baptism signifies two things: the forgiveness of sins and the gift of the Holy Spirit. That is interesting because the two doctrines which challenge the biblical view of baptism today are (1) baptismal regeneration and (2) baptism of the Spirit subsequent to conversion.

But Peter taught neither of these. The "unto (*eis* in Greek) forgiveness" must be understood not in the sense of purpose—as though water itself cleansed our sins—but "on the basis of" forgiveness. Regeneration by water makes no sense here where baptism is so closely coupled with the call to repent.

And the modern doctrine of baptism of the Spirit months or years after conversion is just as alien to the New Testament. The water baptism of the New Testament was itself an announcement that the convert was baptized by the Spirit and thereby spiritually joined to the family of God, the community of the twice born.

After repentance and baptism, these converts were *added* to the church. Jesus and the Apostles knew that seldom, if ever, do decisions survive in a life cut off from the Christian community. Lone Ranger Christians don't make it. These believers were converted to Christ so they were added to the church.

One of the many bright spots in the church growth movement is its stress on "added to the church." Scores of mission leaders are now stressing that evangelism that does not lead to membership in a local church is defective. In our anti-institutional atmosphere that is hard for some people to swallow.

As a young preacher still in Bible school, I used to be troubled by my ministerial colleagues when they reported at our ministers' meetings their latest toll of baptisms and church additions. But I was too spiritual for my own good. I have come to see that their "additions by baptism" were a lot more permanent than my "decisions for Christ."

Vitality of Community

Some critics of the church growth movement have tried to separate quality growth from quantity growth and argue that numbers added to the church are not nearly as important as spiritual growth.

Church growth leaders, however, refuse to accept that kind of artificial divorce because the Bible will not support it. Church growth is like child growth. We want Junior to mature in social awareness and intelligence, but when his weight stays at 83 pounds for three years we get anxious—no matter how smart he gets. Body weight isn't everything but it is a good index of the health of a child. So it is with churches. Additions are an indication of health. Quality and quantity go together. One of the reasons the apostolic church won outsiders to faith in Christ was because Christ was alive and real to the insiders.

Three practices show the vitality of this church: they devoted themselves (1) to the teaching of the Apostles, (2) to the fellowship, and (3) to breaking of bread and the prayers. We might call these discipleship, fellowship, and worship.

This devotion to apostolic teaching is worth noting because churches haven't always been examples of such discipleship. Too often they have turned to some contemporary philosophy or to some socially acceptable values. But the authoritative standard for first-century churches was apostolic teaching. If the vitality of the early Christian communities was maintained by devotion to the Word of God, do we really believe that ours can prosper some other way?

The authority of the Word of God, however, is more than acceptable beliefs. Orthodoxy alone is no guarantee of church growth. Jesus didn't command that we teach believers to *listen* to the Word, but to *observe* it.

If I may call upon Linus again, I think he will make the point better. Lucy finds him making a snowman. She says, "What would you do if I pushed your snowman over?"

"Nothing," says Linus. "What could I do? You're bigger and stronger than I am. You're older. . . . You can run faster. . . . I really couldn't stop you. I realize that I'm at your mercy where things of this sort are concerned. All I can do is simply hope that you will choose not to do so."

Lucy turns away.

And Linus says to the snowman: "Little by little I'm becoming an expert at the soft answer." That is progress. That is spiritual growth.

The vitality of this apostolic church was also evident in its *fellowship*. Few words in the Christian vocabulary today are more abused than *fellowship*. We have come to associate it with a good time in church. We refer to buildings where we play as "fellowship halls." And to times when we eat as "fellowship hours." But in the New Testament, fellowship stood for corporate life in the Spirit. It included giving money to those in need, praying for those who were weak, and crying with those who grieved. Fellowship embraced the whole range of experiences a Christian family has because a Christian fellowship, like a Christian family, shares a common life. It is bound together by birth and kinship.

In his book *The Congregation in Mission* George W. Webber, a pioneer in urban ministries, makes an important observation about fellowship. He notes that many people are currently involved in developing the small group. But he predicts for many of them disillusionment or failure. "When a group is organized for spiritual growth or fellowship or mutual encouragement," Webber writes, "these are objectives that come only as a gift of God and not through the efforts of men. They are desirable by-products, but so subjectively oriented as to lead only to impossible expectations when they are the immediate object of the small group meeting" (New York: Abingdon, 1964, p. 122).

There is a place for small groups in churches, but Webber recommends that their purposes be defined in objective terms that involve work to be done and goals to be achieved, not for fellowship. That strikes me as sound advice.

Perhaps we ought to think more in terms of fellowship linked to evangelism. They aren't really two totally different things, because genuine fellowship reaches out for others and true evangelism enriches and deepens a Christian community.

Notice, finally, that the vitality of this apostolic fellowship was sustained by *worship*. Two expressions—"breaking of bread" and "the prayers"—refer to worship.

Breaking of bread obviously designates a meal, but we may not understand what a meal meant to these people. Near Eastern peoples looked upon eating a meal as a special event. To eat bread with another person created a bond which couldn't be broken—something like smoking the Indian peace pipe. That is why the Pharisees were outraged that Jesus would receive sinners and *eat* with them (Luke 15:1-2). So in the early church, a common meal became not only an emblem but a seal of friendship.

Christians expressed their covenant with each other and with their risen and present Lord by eating together—their love feasts and the Lord's Supper. God was real to them, not just personally, but corporately.

But how about us? Is worship a predictable routine through which we go simply because it is the right day and right hour? Have we regimented and rationalized the mystery of God's presence out of our gatherings? Is the New Covenant, which makes us a special people before God in the world, more than a phrase we use on communion Sundays? Are we really convinced that the living God is the basis of the living church?

Quality of Lifestyle

Churches, like individuals, have personalities. They do things certain ways. They reflect their values and attitudes in their services, their budgets, and their activities.

This apostolic fellowship did too. Notice, the first thing Luke mentions is its *authenticity*. Acts 2:43 indicates that reverential fear came over people as the Apostles gave evidence of God's hand upon them. Jesus had performed miracles to show that the kingdom of God had come with power. Now the Apostles worked miracles to establish their credentials as unique messengers of the kingdom.

God is not likely to work that kind of miracle in our churches. But we still have the problem of establishing authenticity. Pastors and loyal church people are in constant danger of artificiality, of greenhouse Christianity. Our attitudes can easily become humdrum and our words hollow. Artificiality is the first sign of a dying church.

But how do we resist it? I'm convinced that we ought to use wisely the testimonies of people who have a *fresh* experience with God.

I recall one Sunday a few years ago when my pastor began his message by reading a sports story. It was from a suburban newspaper printed a few days earlier, and was titled, "Championship Gym Coach Quits for Ministry Study."

A young coach had led his high school gymastics team in a systematic blitz of the opposition in the state meet and then the next Monday morning had delivered a personal bombshell.

"No, I won't be back at Cherry Creek next year," Coach Edwards told the reporter, confirming rumors which had floated through the state meet on Friday and Saturday nights.

"I start seminary next fall," he said. "I have given this thing a lot of thought and finally made up my mind in December."

"I've really enjoyed working with these kids this year," he said, "but it was always an interim thing with me. I only took the head job on the condition that they find someone else for next year."

The young coach's announcement was the most dramatic event

of the state meet as his heavily favored team jumped out to a substantial lead and finished with 308 points to outdistance their nearest rival at 293.

After the pastor read the story, he called the coach to the pulpit to share how God had dealt with him. In spite of buying a new home, in spite of wanting to start a family after four years of marriage, God had called him—and God would provide. No one asked for evidence of the Gospel that morning!

We ought to notice, too, the *generosity* of this apostolic community (Acts 2:45). Out of their deeply felt unity they gave freely to meet the needs of others. Some have tried to read Communism out of this. But there is no legislation here, no forced communion of goods. This is the spontaneous response of folk who found, "Freely you have received, freely give."

Can you see this happening today in our churches? Not in most of them! We don't allow needs to surface at our meetings. We keep all failings and needs out of sight. The American success cult doesn't tolerate failure so we maintain churches with an antiseptic niceness that denies sin and therefore grace.

But one thing is wrong. A church can never really grow in that kind of environment, because the church exists to serve. In a growing church, people don't ask, "What do I get out of this?" They ask, "What can I give?" And a stranger gets the point. He can feel which attitude is in control.

Finally, notice the *adaptability* of this church. In Acts 2:46 we read that they gathered daily in the temple. That reveals their roots in the past. They continued in their Jewish ways. But the verse also says they broke bread from house to house. That marks the beginning of congregational life in the church.

The new wine of the Gospel was pouring into the old wineskins of Judaism. In time, the skins would break from the expansiveness of new life in Christ. But in the meantime, these believers had the sense not to lose the opportunity for witness and ministry with their relatives and friends. They saw no need to smash tradition under the excitement of their new faith, so they worshiped in the temple *and* in their homes.

Unfortunately, some churches fail to grow because they never learn to adjust to change. They would rather not be bothered! They prefer to sing, "As it was in the beginning, is now, and ever shall be . . ." forgetting that this refers to God, not the church. Tragically, when the security of the familiar becomes our highest value in life, we become idolaters and no longer followers of Jesus Christ.

On the other hand, I have known of "What's Happening Now?" churches. They make idols of the latest fads and innovate the church out of existence.

Churches which grow find a way to relate to change. They don't introduce change simply for the sake of change, but when growth comes they are able to graft new life into the strength of the past and bear even more fruit to the glory of God.

If we expect to produce growing churches, we, too, will have to give ourselves to the intensity of preaching, the integrity of membership, the vitality of genuine community, and the quality of a distinctively Christian lifestyle.

When I summarize a growing church in these four propositions, I sense how woefully inadequate such propositions are. And I remember a story the noted commentator, William Barclay, told in his book, *The Promise of the Spirit*. "A Negro Salvationist was found one day kneeling in front of a table in a church commemorating the conversion there of General Booth. 'O Lord, do it again,' he was praying over and over again. As we read the story of Pentecost and think of the world today and of the impotence of the church, the same prayer will come to our lips, 'O Lord, do it again' " (William Barclay, *The Promise of the Spirit*, Philadelphia: Westminster Press, 1960, pp. 117-118).

5

The Form of the Church

A number of years ago, Joseph Bayly wrote a funny book called *The Gospel Blimp*. It was about a zealous and zany group of Christians who tried to evangelize their neighbors by lofting a blimp over their town with Gospel banners streaming behind it and evangelistic tracts drifting to earth from it. The story was good for laugh after laugh as you read about the blimp's interference with the favorite TV program in town, the *Maxie Belden Show,* and about the Commander's powder blue uniform with shiny gold buttons for public image.

Beneath the humor, however, was an important lesson. Our best attempts to further the Gospel often become the greatest barriers to its acceptance. In terms of the church, the very organizations we create to advance the witness for Christ often pose the greatest obstruction to its reception.

The simple solution would be to avoid all organization. But that is impossible and the New Testament nowhere encourages us to search for a formless fellowship.

The Importance of Form
All life on earth seems to require some sort of form. It is tough to think of formless life. Even a jellyfish has a basic shape. Certainly, in human affairs spirit must express itself in visible

structures before it can make a contribution to the ongoing drama of history.

That is why the church is no disembodied spirit. The Holy Spirit, who is the source of eternal life, is invisible, to be sure, but the church must function in the realm of time and space through visible means.

If Christianity were a philosophy of life, then gurus might travel about informally turning on the light for devoted disciples. But Christianity is more than a moral ideal; it is a movement with a mission.

Lost men must hear the Gospel, so adequately trained witnesses must be sent. The meaning of the Gospel for life must be taught to those who believe, so some form of Christian education must be provided. Christians should express the unity of their faith, so some means of public worship must be developed. The unfortunate and needy must be cared for, so some channels for ministry must be created. In short, if the will of Christ, in even the slightest sense, is to be done on this earth as it is in heaven, the church must be organized in some objective form to manifest itself in those areas in which people live out their lives.

Church history offers us numerous examples of the fact that the church cannot live except as a visibly defined and organized body with a continuing organization. Our Christian past is filled with movements which began as eruptions of spiritual revival, breaking through and revolting against the hardened structure of an older body, and claiming, in the name of the Holy Spirit, liberty from outward forms and institutions. Quakers, Pietists, the Plymouth Brethren, and the Disciples of Christ were among them. History shows how rapidly these movements developed their own forms, their own distinctive customs, beliefs, and organizational structure and forms of government.

If we cannot escape, then, from some organizational form for the church, what help does the New Testament offer us?

Form of the New Testament Churches

A revival movement spreading from Jerusalem to Rome can be traced in the New Testament (Acts 1:8), leaving its Judaistic past farther and farther behind. The old wineskins proved unable to contain the new wine of the Gospel.

Scattered congregations, on the other hand, emerged in the path of the spreading movement, representing the embodiment of the movement in a given place.

We do not know all we would like to know about these early Christians but the general pattern of their life together is clear. The church body met on an appointed day, called the Lord's Day, the first day of the week (Acts 20:7; Rev. 1:10), and under designated leaders they read and studied the Scriptures (1 Tim. 4:13), sang hymns (Col. 3:16), offered prayers to God, and received offerings (1 Cor. 16:1-2). The money was used to help the poor, and the widows (Acts 6:1) as well as to support the leaders (1 Tim. 5:17-18). New converts were added to the church by baptism (Acts 16:33) and the whole church joined in observing the Lord's Supper (1 Cor. 11:17-26).

We can draw only one conclusion from the fragmentary evidence of the New Testament. Apostolic churches were not unstructured, free-lance gatherings for warmhearted believers. They were organized, purposeful assemblies for confessing, baptized disciples. New Testament Christianity is not a formless faith.

At the same time, the New Testament material suggests that while the church must have some organization, no single structure beyond the local congregations is necessary for its existence. Just as no one form of the state makes a state, so no one form of the church makes a church. A state is a valid state if it expresses the organized life of a people at any given time. It may be democratic or republican, a constitutional monarchy or a dictatorship. The particular form does not make the state. The life of a people may express itself in any number of forms. So it is with the church.

The New Testament reveals no uniform church government in the Apostolic Age. According to Acts 13:1-4, the Antioch church had certain charismatic features. Prophets and teachers spoke God's message to the church.

The churches in Asia Minor, under Paul's oversight, probably adopted a style of leadership based on a plurality of elders (Acts 14:23).

Jerusalem retained a loyalty to the family of Jesus and looked to Christ's half brother, James, as a Christian counterpart of the ruler of the synagogue (Acts 15:13). James was succeeded by another half brother, Simeon.

We also know that Titus and Timothy, while not Apostles, assumed a kind of superintendent's role toward some of the congregations under Paul's oversight (Titus 1:5 and Phil. 2:19-24).

Church history, as well as the New Testament, teaches us that the church can and has survived changing times and contrasting cultures by adapting its basic message and mission to changing forms. The final criterion by which to define the church is not a special form, but the Gospel, energized by the Holy Spirit.

In their zeal to restore the New Testament church, some American evangelicals have insisted recently that the New Testament knows only one pattern of church government. The implication is that only those churches with this form are following the Bible completely.

The nature of the church and its mission in the world, revealed to us in the New Testament, must always be our standard. But insistence upon one rigid pattern of government for all local churches and their interchurch structures seems foolhardy for two reasons: first, it focuses attention at the wrong place. It tends to exalt the external organization which the Holy Spirit has used as a vehicle of the Gospel rather than the Gospel itself. A church which does this is in danger of losing the Gospel. Second, it fails to be flexible enough to adapt to the best means of evangelizing in different cultures.

One of the Early Church Fathers of the second century, Irenaeus, caught the New Testament emphasis when he said: "Where the Spirit of God is, there is the church and all grace." Form is essential, for spirit must be embodied. But the Gospel of Christ and the Spirit's presence are more important than the particular forms through which they find expression.

Distortions of the Form of the Church

The New Testament leads us not to a single, rigid organization for the churches for all times but to basic principles arising from the Gospel and the nature of the church as a redeemed community. From these two sources, the Gospel and the church, we can recognize two distortions of the form of the church: institutionalism, on the one hand, and individualism, on the other.

Institutionalists, those who elevate some organizational form as the mark of the true church, tend to lay great stress on the relation of the official ministry to the existence of the church. To them, the church *is* the ministry, whether pope, bishop, elders, or pastor-teachers. The church is less the people of God than it is an official class of ministers through whom church members find their relation to God established. Mediation of God's grace is vital.

A few years ago, I heard Kenneth Chafin, a prominent Southern Baptist pastor, tell about a church business meeting. The pastor stood and said, "This recommendation comes as a recommendation of the personnel committee, the finance committee and the board of deacons. The church staff has voted unanimously for it. We feel it is the will of God. Are there any questions?"

That is institutionalism with a smile.

The classic answer to this position is the doctrine of the priesthood of believers. Even in the Old Testament, Israel as a people was the priesthood. At Mount Sinai, when the Ten Commandments were given, God spoke to all the people saying, "You shall be to Me a kingdom of priests and a holy nation" (Ex. 19:6, RSV). Only practical purposes dictated that one group be set aside in Israel as a priestly class (Num. 3:12-13).

The New Testament recognizes only one priest, Jesus Christ. He was the one chosen to make the final and perfect offering to God for the people. He presented Himself as the sacrificial Lamb (Heb. 7:26-27; 1 Peter 1:18-19) and removed forever any necessity for priests in the literal sense. That is why the New Testament never uses the term *priest* to designate a special class of officials in the church. No such officials are needed.

All references to sacrifice and offerings within the church are spiritualized and are performed by the whole body. Peter's use of the Old Testament description of Israel is typical: "You [plural] are a chosen race, a royal priesthood, a holy nation, God's own people" (1 Peter 2:9, RSV). Indwelt by the Spirit, the church now fulfills the role of priesthood in the world.

The popular idea of a mediatorial priesthood is alien to both the letter and the spirit of the New Testament. It is a return to a legalism that we fallen men find attractive, whether we call ourselves Catholics or Protestants. We are forever in danger of looking for leaders who will give us all the answers and provide a better security than that found in a community of faith under the authority of the Word of God. That is our propensity but it isn't God's provision.

In the United States, Christians have tended to counter the threat of institutionalism with another distortion: individualism.

In individualism, the believing individual is all important. Outward forms and corporate institutions of the visible church tend to be of secondary importance. The church is essentially a fellowship of persons who have faith in Christ. Almost any small group of believing individuals can be called the church.

The strength of individualism lies in the truth that the church does not make the believing individuals what they are; they are what they are by the grace and power of God. The part does come before the whole in the sense that without the parts there would be no whole. Individualism suffers, however, from some fundamental weaknesses. In its protest of institutionalism, it falls before the perils of subjectivity.

First is the peril of an independence which loses sight of the unity in Christ. Spiritual freedom so speedily degenerates into something local and sectarian. As important as the gathering together for fellowship is, it has never been the whole truth about the church. The church is also called to worship and mission.

Second is the peril of a perfectionism that so easily becomes the sin of spiritual pride, and ends as the sin of schism. I think here of Calvin's striking words in defense of the ordinary people of a parish or city who make no high claim to be "righteous overmuch." To remain loyal to the New Testament, the local church must participate in the life of the church at large. An "independent" church is a contradiction because it is a denial of the unity of the Spirit.

Paul, who stressed so often the integrity of the local church, was careful to counteract any tendency toward isolation of those churches he helped to establish. The letter that contains most evidence of this is 1 Corinthians. He sounds the keynote against independency in his opening greeting: "Paul . . . to the church of God which is at Corinth . . . called to be saints, together with all those who in every place call on the name of our Lord Jesus Christ" (1:1-2, RSV).

Having placed the fundamental teaching before the Corinthians, Paul repeatedly applied it to practical matters in the letter. The problem of allowing unveiled women to pray in public is a good example. He condemned the Corinthian practice by referring to the practices of other churches. We recognize no such practice, he says, "nor do the churches of God" (1 Cor. 11:16, RSV). Clearly, Paul expected the Corinthian congregation to bear in mind appropriate Christian practice elsewhere.

The Case for Denominations

This brings us to the ways in which churches in modern times have sought to express the unity of the Spirit beyond the local church.

Since the fundamentalist struggle with modernism in the 1920s, the term *denomination* has not been in favor among many conservative evangelicals. That is unfortunate, for it originally stood for an important principle—cooperation with other Christians without compromise of fundamental convictions.

The idea goes back to a minority wing of the Puritan party in 17th-century England. At the Westminster Assembly (1643) was a group of Independents akin to American Congregationalists. These men had come to the conclusion that the sinful condition of man, even Christian men, made the full and clear grasp of the truth of God an impossibility. Consequently, no single body of beliefs can ever fully represent God's total demand upon the minds and hearts of believers and no single body of Christians can claim to be the true church of God without considering other believers in other groups.

Thus, in the minds of these Puritans, the word *denomination* implied that a particular body of Christians (let us say, for example, the Baptists) was only a portion of the total Christian church, called—or denominated—by its particular name, Baptist.

The denominational idea of the church originally stood for an important biblical truth. The church is one. There is only one Saviour, only one Gospel, only one Spirit, so there can be only one church. Divisions, therefore, must be *within* the one body, not *from* the body. Otherwise, Christ Himself would be divided and that is unthinkable (1 Cor. 1:12-13).

Exulting in this denominational theory, the Rev. Albert Barnes, the distinguished Presbyterian minister and Bible commentator, declared in 1840, "The spirit of this land is, that the Church of Christ is not under the Episcopal form, or the Baptist, the Methodist, the Presbyterian, or the Congregational form exclusively; all are to all intents and purposes, to be recognized as parts of the one holy catholic church." Most 19th-century evangelicals, at least before the Civil War, would have agreed.

From the denominational concept, then, many Christians learned how to cooperate within the fundamental truths of God and His redemption through Jesus Christ, while remaining denominationally loyal to the doctrines regarding the church and the Christian life—without compromise. Denominational differences may not be primary, but they are not therefore *adiaphora*, "matters of indifference."

The weaknesses of the denominational form of the church appear from two directions. A denomination can claim a monopoly on the grace of God and look on other Christians as spiritually inferior. That weakness we call sectarianism.

On the other hand, a denomination can seek Christian unity so zealously that it surrenders essential biblical truth. Charles Schultz's Linus expressed this mood best when he said, "It doesn't matter what you believe so long as you're sincere." That is the weakness of indifferentism.

Basic Types of Government

Within the denominational concept of the church, three major types of organization can be found. The first is the episcopal type. This type lays great stress on the historic episcopate, or the continuation of a class of superior clergy—bishops. They are the guardians of tradition, and the final authorities in the life of the church. Some adherents of this form insist that the existence of the church depends on the historic episcopate. "No bishop, no church." For others it is simply desirable for the health of the church, the best way for the church to govern itself.

The second type is presbyterial, or representative. In this type, all ministers are on the same level. Authority is vested in representatives chosen by the people, both ministerial and lay, who act in their name. The local church is governed by the pastor, or pastors if there be more than one, and elders elected by the congregation. At all levels above the local church, the representatives who act for the church are evenly divided between clergy and laymen, thus demonstrating their equality.

The third type is congregational, or democratic. Like the presbyterial form, the congregational knows only one level of clergymen. Authority, however, is not vested in chosen representatives who act for the people, but lies in the direct action of the people themselves. The church exists in the local congregation. It is united with other congregations not organically, but on the basis of voluntary fellowship, from which the local church may withdraw at any time, and still remain a church. The original intent of the congregational form was to permit the direct leadership of the Holy Spirit in each local church.

A fourth type is one in which all possible external form is abandoned in the interests of giving free play to the immediate leadership of the Holy Spirit. The Quakers are representative of this type. The ministry, the sacraments, and all stated forms of worship are abandoned. Even the Bible is made secondary to the "inner light" of the Holy Spirit's direct guidance.

This fourth type of government has never been widely accepted in the church. It fails to stress sufficiently the fact that in the present world, forms are necessary for spirit to express itself. The episcopal system is not based on the Scriptures, but on the developing tradition in the early church. Both the presbyterial and congregational forms, however, claim scriptural support. Where the weight of Scripture lies would be determined largely by the pre-suppositions held by each side of the debate.

The Parachurch Agencies

Under the impact of theological liberalism in the early years of the 20th century, traditional differences in church government among evangelicals tended to get lost beneath weightier matters of doctrine.

The form of cooperation through which many evangelicals came to express their interest in evangelistic or social reforms was the interdenominational voluntary society. In recent years, we have adopted the label, "parachurch" agency.

In the 19th century, these were groups of individual Christians—mostly from the churches but under no church authority—who joined together in societies for the preaching of the Gospel or for some ministry of mercy.

Once adopted in America, these societies made possible a quick response to spiritual needs and an effective means of marshalling support. Individuals from various denominations could share in the efforts without raising the troublesome questions surrounding the nature and mission of the church.

Voluntary societies channeled the energy generated by the fires of revival into missionary, educational, and reform causes. Active in America prior to the Civil War were the American Home Missionary Society, the American Education Society, the American Temperance Society, the American Tract Society, the American Peace Society, the American Sunday School Union, and scores of others. Orestes Brownson, a New England minister, complained that "matters have come to such a pass, that a peaceable man can hardly venture to eat or drink, to go to bed or get up, to correct his children or kiss his wife" without the sanction or direction of some society.

In the 1920s, when the fundamentalists lost the struggle for control of several of the larger denominations, they turned to the existing interdenominational agencies and created still others in order to fulfill their educational, missionary, and social service ministries.

In this way, fundamentalists and evangelicals came to rely almost exclusively on the voluntary society pattern of cooperation. Youth for Christ, Inter-Varsity Christian Fellowship, the Christian Business Men's Committee, and numerous other organizations followed the earlier plan.

The advantages of the parachurch form of cooperation were not hard to find. For centuries, Christians had differed over various details of the doctrine of the church such as baptism, ordination, and the meaning of the Lord's Supper. Sidestepping all these issues, the voluntary societies appealed directly to individuals for support, both financial and personal. This maneuver allowed them to evangelize or to distribute literature or to establish orphanages without checking with church authorities.

Parachurch agencies, however, have suffered from the lack of biblical precedent and have often been victims of individualism. Sometimes, powerful leaders have built religious kingdoms; sometimes, loyalty to an agency has displaced loyalty to the church, creating not parachurch agencies but antichurch agencies.

When we survey the various forms of the church beyond the local level—as we have in this chapter—we see how readily they become "Gospel blimps." They are designed to advance the witness for Christ, but they often obscure that witness. The only solution, it seems, is continual renewal of our organizational structures according to biblical standards and evangelistic needs. Beyond that we can give thanks that God uses "earthen vessels."

6

Membership in the Church

A number of years ago, while engaged in a campus ministry, I was teaching a class of young Christians about the basics of the Christian life. A coed named Karen stayed behind after class to pursue a point I had made. She had recently made a decision for Christ but she wasn't sure that it was necessary to follow through with baptism and church membership.

I can still remember the look on Karen's face as I used an analogy I have used many times since.

"What is marriage, Karen?" I asked her.

She smiled because she was already taking serious steps in that direction. "Well, it's love, I guess."

"So is being a Christian," I said. "It is a personal relationship between you and the Lord Jesus Christ. But is marriage anything else?"

"Sure," she responded, "it is a wedding ceremony." And her eyes glistened, revealing warm thoughts of her own wedding.

"Of course," I said. "What is real love without the vows that protect love and make it permanent in the sight of God and men? So it is with being a Christian. It has a personal side, but it also has a ceremonial side. Baptism is that ceremony, followed by church membership. It can't create love but it can make it responsible and public."

Karen got the point. But her struggle is a common one.

For most Christians, the first place the church-in-theory meets the church-in-fact is in church membership. Few believers realize how much time Satan spends at the door of the church. It is as though he senses a major battle here for people who have made "a decision for Christ."

C. S. Lewis recognized this in his correspondence from Screwtape. "My dear Wormwood," he writes, "I note with grave displeasure that your patient has become a Christian. . . . There is no need to despair. . . . One of your great allies at present is the Church itself. . . . All your patient sees is the half-finished, sham Gothic erection on the new building estate. . . . When he gets to his pew and looks around him he sees just that selection of his neighbours whom he has hitherto avoided. You want to lean pretty heavily on those neighbours. . . . At his present stage, you see, he has an idea of 'Christians' in his mind which he supposes to be spiritual but which, in fact, is largely pictorial."

Is it the trick of Satan to keep us looking for something higher than a local community of ordinary believers in Christ? If division in Christian ranks is Satan's goal he has succeeded more than once on this front. Church people can't even agree on the meaning of their membership.

Positions on Church Membership

Three basic positions on this question can be found among church people.

The view held by most Christians could be called the institutional Christian view. This position has been around a long time. Many Roman Catholics, Lutherans, and Reformed Christians hold it today. Basically, it looks on the church as a community in which people become Christians. We might compare it to a school of nursing which takes young women and men who know nothing about the care of patients or the combating of disease. Over a period of years, the school educates and trains these young people till they receive their cap and license certifying that they are, in fact, nurses.

Institutional Christians believe that God established the church and provided it with special grace for the salvation of men, women, and children. This grace is distributed to church members through the sacraments of the church. These sacraments are special ceremonies ordained by God for the church to observe in order to educate and train church members in the Christian life.

The first sacrament a church member can receive is baptism. In fact, according to institutional Christians, it is baptism that makes (or begins to make) a person a Christian. Since God's saving grace comes to a person through the sacrament, most institutional Christians believe that even babies can receive baptism and profit from it. It provides a kind of preliminary membership. Later, somewhere around 10 or 12 years of age, the child must receive instruction in the meaning of the Christian faith and be received into full membership by receiving his first communion (Lord's Supper).

Through these, and other ceremonies and classes, institutional Christians are seeking to teach their children and other people that the church is God's school of Christianity, the only established institution for training in righteousness.

A second view of church membership is held by Christians whom we might call baptistic Christians. The name is not altogether proper because it suggests that only Baptists accept this view. While Baptists do hold it and are probably the largest group to do so, many other Christians also believe and practice it. Among these are many Pentecostal and Bible churches. The name, at any rate, is not nearly as important for our purposes as the idea.

The basic view of church membership held by these Christians is more exclusive in the sense that membership is reserved for those who can attest to their personal faith in Jesus Christ and are willing to express that faith in Gospel baptism. It is necessary to call it Gospel baptism because these Christians believe that the church and baptism stand for something other than a school in Christianity and the act of enrolling in it.

Baptistic Christians believe that the church is more like a family than a school. You do not enroll in families; you are added to a family by birth. Thus, baptistic Christians insist that a person must be born again in order to be added to the church, the family of God. Further, baptism is not the birth but is a reenactment of the Gospel by which the believer becomes a child of God. Thus, baptistic Christians try to reserve baptism and church membership for men, women, and children who have personal faith in Jesus Christ.

A third view of church membership is held by a small minority of Christians we might call nonmembership Christians. No major denomination holds this view, but many independent Christians believe it. They hold that a Christian may be baptized if he wishes, but his personal faith has already made him a member of the true church. No outward act will add to that. And since the inward decision is the sole requirement in God's eyes, the outward mode of baptism is unimportant. It may be sprinkling, immersion, pouring, or nothing.

From these positions it is clear that Christians concerned about following New Testament teachings face two questions: Is there such a thing as church membership in the New Testament? If there is, what is the relationship between baptism and church membership?

The first question calls for a definition of terms. What do we mean by church membership? Do we mean a church roll? A certificate of membership? Or a responsible relationship with a specific group?

The New Testament habitually makes a distinction between groups of Christians moving about the Mediterranean world and churches located in certain places. Furthermore, the New Testament sees nothing unspiritual about keeping rolls. According to Luke 10:20 it is done in heaven. There is even evidence that the early churches also kept rolls—at least, of some of their widows (1 Tim. 5:9, 11). The New Testament writings also indicate that something like church letters were used to commend a believer to a church. On various occasions, Paul commended Timothy (1 Cor. 16:10), Titus (2 Cor. 8:23), Phoebe (Rom. 16:1), and Mark (Col. 4:10).

No one, of course, should argue that first-century practices were exactly like our own. To my knowledge, no first-century church membership roll has survived. But, surely, the New Testament does offer enough evidence to challenge the nonmembership view.

The tough love taught to New Testament Christians required church membership because it was the kind of love that assumed responsibility for brothers and sisters. It was not a matter of words in general offered to Christians in general. It was love that submitted to other members out of reverence for Christ and valued leaders who looked after the souls of those in the body (Heb. 13:17).

Some time ago, *Moody Monthly* magazine made an appropriate observation about a hitchhiker. He is an interesting character. He wants a free ride. He assumes no responsibility for the money needed to purchase the car, the gas to run it or the cost of maintenance. He expects a comfortable ride and adequate safety. He assumes the driver has insurance covering him in case of an accident. He thinks nothing of requesting that he be taken to a certain place even though it means extra miles or inconvenience to his host.

There is a situation, however, even worse. Consider the person who demands all the benefits and privileges of the church without feeling the slightest responsibility for its support in money, time or service. And if he does not get all he thinks is his by some natural right, he is usually the most demanding and critical. He too is a hitchhiker.

The New Testament, however, knows no hitchhikers in the kingdom because the love the Gospel brings is responsible—even to the exercise of discipline in the churches. Of all the practices of the apostolic churches, surely discipline argues most convincingly for church membership. How could a brother or sister be expelled from a church fellowship if there was no membership?

In his book, *Worship in the Early Church,* Professor Ralph P. Martin surveys the New Testament material on the inner life of the church and he concludes: "If the early church had been a society of free-thinkers in which every one was at liberty to believe what he thought acceptable and to live as he pleased, with no guiding lines of doctrine and ethical behaviour patterns, the New Testament Letters would be far different from what we know them" (*Worship in the Early Church*, Grand Rapids: Eerdmans, 1975, p. 55).

Most churches have been persuaded by this line of argument. There is nothing unspiritual about church membership. On the contrary, the only way to minister to and through the visible church on earth is to have some means of identifying who is in and who is not in it—leaving all exceptional cases with God.

Whatever value the idea of the invisible church outside the visible church may have for theological purposes, in dealing with visible congregations, it is of little worth.

This leaves us with a choice between two kinds of visible churches. There are those visible churches that find their identity in some kind of institutional structure: the proper ordination, the correct doctrine, or the valid sacrament. Churchmen tend to give less attention to the quality of membership when visibility rests in these institutional forms. Without adequate care for members' spiritual condition, the question often arises, "When will the world overwhelm the church?"

Other visible churches seek to maintain a converted membership. Their concern for the quality of church membership means that these churches face the problem of distinguishing between wheat that looks like tares and tares that look like wheat.

The New Testament itself, however, appears to support the practice of church membership and the requirement of personal faith in Christ as a prerequisite. While no clear examples of New Testament church rolls survive, the attitude toward the church gathered in local assemblies is such that relationships to the local body of believers were responsible ones.

Let's turn, then, to the second basic question: What is the relationship of baptism to church membership?

Questions surrounding baptism come from all directions. In American evangelical circles, it is necessary to start with certain objections to water baptism.

Objections to Baptism

Under the impact of revivalism, with its heavy stress on genuine personal conversions, many evangelicals have come to question the value of water baptism. It is Christ, they say, who saves through faith alone; not the church through ceremonies. These believers base their case on three arguments drawn from the New Testament.

A distinction between true spirituality and water baptism is nearly always made. The argument often appeals to Jesus' promise of the coming baptism. Jesus said, "John truly baptized with water; but ye shall be baptized with the Holy Spirit not many days hence" (Acts 1:5; see also John's own promise, Mark 1:8 and Luke 3:16).

Is this, in fact, support for a waterless Christian baptism? It is clear that a contrast is intended: John's baptism with water and Jesus' promised baptism with the Holy Spirit. John's disciples knew only a baptism unto repentance marked by water; Jesus' disciples would know more than a baptism unto repentance; they would know a baptism of the Spirit.

But does this baptism with the Spirit exclude water as a symbol or instrument of the Spirit? Clearly not, because the Book of Acts shows that believers received the Spirit and were baptized in water. The text, then, is not contrasting water and Spirit as much as it is contrasting the baptism John practiced with Christian baptism.

A second argument some evangelicals use to depreciate the value of water baptism rests upon Paul's remark to the Corinthian church: "I thank God that I baptized none of you. . . . Christ sent me not to baptize, but to preach the Gospel" (1 Cor. 1:14, 17).

The argument, again, insists that Paul minimized the importance of baptism and stressed the significance of preaching and receiving the Gospel. But this argument is fallacious. Paul was not opposing baptism *per se*. He argued that baptism is the basis of the church's unity! (v. 13) The problem is not baptism; the problem is false loyalty to baptizers such as Paul, Apollos, and Peter, the men the Corinthian parties were admiring and around whom they were gathering.

A third argument some evangelicals often use rests on a special understanding of the body of Christ. They maintain that it is not necessary to be baptized to be added to the body of Christ, so why should we make higher demands than God makes?

If, by this argument, these evangelicals are intending to stress the fact that baptism is not the constituting element in the body of Christ, they are probably right. But their argument misses the point. Neither baptism nor faith provides the basis of the body. The total number of members do not constitute the body of Christ. The body of Christ is based on Christ Himself and the Spirit He gives creates the unity of the body (see 1 Cor. 12:12-13).

But this truth—the divine essence of the church—is never used in the New Testament to dismiss baptism or responsible church-manship in the visible church on earth. On the contrary, this doctrine is used in 1 Corinthians 12 to counteract divisions in the local assembly created by rivalries over spiritual gifts.

The New Testament provides no real support for those who try to diminish the proper place of baptism by appealing to a super-spirituality. These devout evangelicals, seeking to avoid any idea of water itself producing new life (baptismal regeneration), make salvation more pietistic than does the New Testament.

The Meaning of Baptism

If we cannot justifiably dismiss baptism altogether, we must go on to ask its true meaning. Here, again, Christians differ. Some say it means the washing away of original sin. The water actually has the power to bring spiritual life, even to an infant.

Personally, I find in the New Testament no link between the removal of original sin and the application of water. The whole idea of a special priesthood empowered by ordination to dispense saving grace—which is often the basis of this view of baptism—is a later concept of the ministry. It is too highly institutional to belong to the Apostles.

Other Christians argue that baptism is the sign of the covenant. It is, they say, the New Testament alternative to Old Testament circumcision. It marks one's membership within the people of God and includes not only the believing parents but also their children. Since baptism does not indicate the presence of personal saving faith but God's promise of the blessings of faith, an infant may be included. He may later become a believer or he may not, depending on his own will.

While this position has the advantage of stressing the unity of the people of God in Scripture, it faces at least two major obstructions. First, there is no explicit instance in the New Testament of an infant baptism. And, second, the practice of baptism in both Jewish proselyte baptism and the baptism of John the Baptist required the candidate's understanding of the meaning of his baptism. The link between circumcision and baptism, as some have argued, was certainly not self-evident.

Still other Christians hold that baptism depicts the personal acceptance by faith of the new life offered to us by Jesus Christ. In a word, they hold to believer's baptism. While I understand how other Christians can hold other views, this position, it seems to me, has more biblical support.

Probably no one can adequately explain the full meaning of baptism as the apostolic churches practiced it, but three ideas seem to appear again and again.

First, baptism is a symbolic expression of acceptance of the Gospel. The New Testament consistently links the ceremony with a presentation of the Good News about Jesus and with a believer's repentance and faith. "We glean from the record in the Acts of the Apostles," Professor Martin writes, "that conversion and baptism were regarded as the inside and outside of the same experience" (*Worship in the Early Church*, p. 60).

The fullest account of a New Testament baptism is that of the Ethiopian eunuch (Acts 8:26-38). The eunuch was reading the great prophetic Scripture, Isaiah 53. "Whom is the prophet talking about?" he asked Philip. This gave Philip the opportunity he wanted, and beginning "at the same Scripture" (and where better could he begin?), "he preached unto him Jesus." There must have been some reference to baptism in their conversation for when they came to some water, the eunuch asked, "Why shouldn't I be baptized?" To which Philip replied, "If you believe with all your heart you may." And he answered Philip, "I believe that Jesus Christ is the Son of God." So the chariot was halted, "and both Philip and the eunuch went down into the water and Philip baptized him." Philip's reply to the eunuch's question about the terms of baptism is not part of the original text of the narrative, as a number of the modern translations note, but it undoubtedly represents the mind of the Early Church, and the eunuch's question must have been answered in some such way as is suggested.

This and other shorter passages make clear that the most fundamental truth depicted in the act of baptism is the spiritual union of the believer with the Lord Jesus in His death, burial, and resurrection. To be "in Christ" means to share spiritually in the saving acts of Jesus. The believer has died to his old life, his past is buried, and he has been raised with Christ to a new life under the Spirit's control (Rom. 6:3-4; Col. 2:12).

When Peter's hearers on the Day of Pentecost cried out, "What shall we do?" he told them to repent of their sins and be baptized in the name of Jesus. He indicated that baptism speaks of forgiveness of sins and the gift of the Spirit (Acts 2:38). Baptism, he said, symbolizes two spiritual realities: A believer's freedom from guilt, because Jesus died; and his power for a new life, because Jesus was raised and sent His Spirit. Theologically, we can say baptism depicts justification by faith in Jesus' blood and sanctification by faith in the power of His resurrection life.

Second, baptism is the evidence of a moral cleansing. The link between the use of water and the experience of cleansing from sin is a natural one. "Arise and be baptized," Ananias told Paul, "and wash away your sins, calling on the name of the Lord" (Acts 22:16). And later, Paul, in making a moral appeal to the Corinthians, reminded them that the unrighteous will not inherit the kingdom of God—"and such were some of you, but you were washed" (1 Cor. 6:11).

Baptism is not itself the means of cleansing; it is the sign of it. The cleansing that baptism expresses is moral and is a work of the Holy Spirit within a believer.

The baptism of a believer in water is, however, extremely important. Baptism as a public act takes the inward experience of cleansing and gives it concrete expression. What may appear to be a passing mood of the convert, a moment of excitement, becomes a public event that no changing emotion can afterward erase.

Baptism thus lifts faith out of the uncertain sands of inward religious moods and roots it in an act of commitment and obedience. Faith, the convert learns, is not simply a private opinion; it is a life of discipleship in the will of God.

Finally, baptism is an act of initiation. Union with Christ means union with His people. Early Christians were familiar with the initiation ideas of Judaism, if not those of pagan religions, and they almost certainly considered baptism as the Christian initiation ceremony. Paul pointed in this direction when he wrote, "We were all baptized by one Spirit into one body—whether Jews or Gentiles, slave or free" (1 Cor. 12:13). In this sense, baptism is the door into the church. By means of it men and women are united in one body, the confessional fellowship of all who love the Lord Jesus, and therefore in the local assembly.

7

Worship and the Church

In his book *Church—Who Needs It?* David Allan Hubbard reminds us that all the world loves a holiday. It would be hard, he says, to go any place or find any people without holidays. "For some, holidays are tied to the seasons, like the great midsummer festivities in Scandinavia or the midwinter carnivals in Minnesota. For others, holidays remember great historical events, especially days of independence or liberation from tyranny, like Bastille Day in France, Cinco de Mayo in Mexico, or the Fourth of July in the United States" (Glendale: Regal Books, 1974, p. 14).

Though all the world loves a holiday, there is no holiday that is really worldwide. Most of them are rooted in national or tribal traditions or tied to the history of a specific group. In a sense, holidays are in-group celebrations that have little or no significance elsewhere.

The nearest thing to a worldwide holiday is a day we have come to take for granted—Sunday. In spite of the mounting tide of secularization in the Western world during the last two centuries, Sunday is observed by more people than any other holy day known to man. Christians have been doing it for two thousand years because they find the meaning of life in weekly worship of Jesus Christ, "the firstborn of the dead." An unknown poet once wrote:

Of all the prizes
That earth can give,
This is the best:
To find Thee, Lord,
A living presence near,
And in Thee rest.

This longing within a Christian congregation sets it off from all other human gatherings. Others meet for pleasure, or study, or to plot a course of action. The church meets to worship.

Worship may involve enjoyment, instruction, and plans for action—but the heart of the matter is always the fact of God, and the relationship of the worshipers to Him. The joy of the worshiper is in God. His instruction is in the will of God. His plans for action are in the purposes of God. It is the centrality of God that makes worship what it is.

The Meaning of Christian Worship

Worship is the act of the assembled church in which praise and honor are directed to God for His gracious gifts to His people in and through Jesus Christ. The key to true worship is not man; it is God. The God of the Bible has so revealed Himself to us that the nature of Christian worship is determined by His character.

The Bible teaches us that God searches for men who will worship Him in spirit and in truth (John 4:23) and that He has removed forever the barriers to communion with Him. True Christian worship, then, is not something man does for God; it is our grateful acceptance of what God has already done for us in the death and resurrection of Jesus Christ.

Biblical worship is unique. The forms of worship used by Israel in Old Testament times were outwardly similar to the forms of worship used by the nations around them, but the inner meaning was vastly different. The pagans initiated their acts of worship themselves, in the hope of doing something to gain the favor of the gods. Hebrew worship was a response to what God had already done for them. It was not designed to gain God's favor. It was simply the glad recognition that a loving God had already, on His own initiative, offered His mercy and grace.

Worship, as the grateful acceptance of God's grace, is nearly always accompanied by praise and adoration.

I was glad when they said to me,
"Let us go to the house of the Lord"
(Ps. 122:1, RSV).

O give thanks to the Lord, for He is good;
His steadfast love endures for ever
(Ps. 118:1, RSV).

This note is characteristic of biblical worship. Phrases like "Praise the Lord," "O sing to the Lord," and "Rejoice in the Lord" run like golden threads through the worship of the Bible. Praise and adoration are simply the believer's response to God. Since God is Creator, Redeemer, and Lord, the people of God bow before Him in adoration and thanksgiving, recognizing that life and all good gifts come from His hand. To acknowledge God as Creator and Redeemer is to glorify God; it is to magnify His supreme worth.

Unfortunately, too many of us are guilty of the late Peter Taylor Forsyth's charge: "Instead of placing themselves at the service of God, most people want a God who is at their service" (*The Cure of Souls: An Anthology of P. T. Forsyth's Practical Writings,* edited by Harry Escott, Grand Rapids: Eerdmans, 1971, p. 59).

True worship, however, not only acknowledges God by lips but also by lives. Isaiah assures us that "They that wait upon the Lord shall renew their strength" (Isa. 40:31). Far from offering an escape from the world, biblical worship leads us into the world in grateful, obedient action.

The focus of our corporate worship, however, must always be the glory of God. In modern worship services, too much attention is directed toward what happens to the worshiper. Churches resort to sound, lighting, symbolism, liturgy, and pageantry to produce emotional feelings in the worshiper. Those who participate tend to evaluate the service in terms of how it lifted them up or gave them a good feeling or inspired them.

We need to be alert here. It is possible to confuse entertainment with worship, to substitute what someone has called "subjective affection" for "objective trust." We can mistake the aesthetic enjoyment we get from a selection by the choir, or the architectural beauty of a church building, for a true worship experience.

C. S. Lewis put it best when he wrote, "A good shoe is a shoe you don't notice. Good reading becomes possible when you need not consciously think about eyes or light, or print, or spelling. The perfect church service would be one we were almost unaware of; our attention would have been on God" (*Letters to Malcolm,* New York: Harcourt, Brace, and World, 1964, p. 4).

American evangelicals, it seems to me, face another corruption of true worship. As a doctrinal movement, they often regard the presentation of some new truths from the Bible as a blessing in worship. This turns worship into an intellectual experience. Biblical worship is not mindless—as Paul argued in 1 Corinthians 14—but the God we worship will always be greater than our thoughts, even about the Bible. The Book of Job teaches us that God is near even during those times when we have reason to doubt that He loves us. His ways are beyond our understanding.

To evaluate worship by what happens to the worshiper is to make men, not God, the center of worship. This is to use God for human ends. But it is not God's chief end to glorify man and to make him happy forever. It is rather man's chief end to glorify God, and to enjoy Him forever. And this is the primary purpose of all true worship.

The Necessity for Corporate Worship

The corporate character of salvation which we discussed in chapter 3 relates especially to worship. Worship is not a solo, it is a chorus. It is the family of God gathered in His presence to glorify Him, each believer assembling with other believers to realize the oneness of the people of God. "Let us consider how we may spur one another on toward love and good deeds" says the apostolic witness. "Let us not give up meeting together, as some are in the habit of doing, but let us encourage one another" (Heb. 10:24-25, NIV).

This is not merely the opinion of one New Testament writer, nor the advice of an ambitious minister who wants a good attendance record for his annual report. It is the expression of the corporate nature of the church. To be saved means that we belong to the company of the saved. John Calvin saw this clearly when he wrote: "Apart from the body of Christ, and the fellowship of the godly, there can be no hope of reconciliation with God."

The Holy Spirit was given not to isolated individuals, but to the church. If we have the gift of the Holy Spirit, we are vitally joined in the fellowship of the body to whom the Holy Spirit is given. Outside this body there is no salvation. To fail to worship with God's people regularly and to share in the life of the people of God, yet to claim to be a Christian, is a flat contradiction in terms. Whatever the exceptions to this rule, they only confirm the fact that exceptional cases do not destroy the rule. They usually reveal someone's lack of understanding of his own faith. "All who believed were together" is the earliest description of the church (Acts 2:44, RSV) and is an abiding mark of the church's life in all generations.

Ritual in Worship

Worship in the church raises the question of the place of ritual, "the form or forms of conducting worship." The congregation can scarcely avoid some ritual. The differences in churches usually involve the amount and types.

Someone has called ritual "God's table manners." That is helpful. It reminds us that we should approach God in an orderly and mannerly fashion.

Three cautions, however, need to be underscored. First, though table manners are good, they should not stifle the members. In the intimacies of the home, rudeness never has a place, but everyone should feel the warmth of acceptance. Too much rigid formality turns a family into a gathering of stilted acquaintances.

In his essay on manners, Ralph Waldo Emerson insists that the best manners grow out of absolute sincerity. He argued that one could get down on the floor and play with a child in the drawing room and still be well mannered if he were sincere in the act. To be well mannered in God's house does not always mean to follow printed forms with exactness. It means the free and sincere expression of love, and glad outflow of communion with God in whatever forms are best suited to the occasion.

Since corporate worship includes the whole church family, individuals in the group must control their individuality to avoid offending others. Confusion and chaos do not glorify God. The "manifestation of the Spirit," said Paul, is given "for the common good" (1 Cor. 12:7). In a body, the feet, hands, ears, and eyes must be coordinated so that they can function in unity. Paul counseled, "Let all things be done for edification . . . so that all may learn and all be encouraged. . . . For God is not a God of confusion but of peace" (1 Cor. 14:26, 31, 33, RSV).

Within the limits of dignity worthy of the presence of God, however, we should be free at any time to set aside or change our stated ritual under the leadership of the Holy Spirit. Table manners, yes; but not the rigid type that stifle the intimate fellowship of the family of God.

A second caution about ritual is that good manners which are external, but do not express the true feelings of the hearts, become hypocrisy. They degrade rather than exalt human relationships. Likewise, religious ritual performed with external correctness but merely to maintain a long-standing tradition, becomes a religious show which God hates. Isaiah voiced God's judgment on those who "honor Me with their lips, while their hearts are far from Me" (Isa. 29:13). Jesus declared that God preferred the open rebellion of the publicans and harlots to the showy religious exercises of the Pharisees (Matt. 21:31).

For generations, ritual has often been substituted for heart religion. Again and again, the prophets denounced ritual which had no religious reality behind it. "What to Me is the multitude of your sacrifices?" cried God through Isaiah. "I have had enough of burnt offerings of rams and the fat of fed beasts" (Isa. 1:11, RSV). Ritual can become a cloak for sin.

Jesus struck the same note when He said to men who were meticulous about ritual observance, "Go and learn what this means, 'I desire mercy, and not sacrifice'" (Matt. 9:13, RSV).

The prophets and Jesus were not ruling ritual out of the life of God's people. They were saying that when ritual ceases to express the heart relationship of the worshiper to God, it becomes a barrier rather than an aid, a shield to hide the soul's true condition rather than the means of approach to God. We must continually examine our worship services to make them channels of true devotion rather than substitutes for it.

A third caution concerning ritual is that it must be used to reveal God's grace rather than something done by man or in the name of man. In the Book of Exodus, worship followed redemption and law. First, God acted in behalf of man when he was helpless to do anything for himself. This is grace—God's free and undeserved action for man's deliverance. Second, came the giving of the Law. This was the way man was to show his gratitude—obedience to God in life. Finally, the Lord instituted worship. It was designed to remind the people of God's redemption, to depict the fact that He was their ever-present Redeemer, to give them some means of expressing their gratitude for their salvation, and to prompt their obedience to God's will.

This is the purpose of ritual, however much or little of it we use in worship. It is designed as an orderly means of reminding us of God's redeeming mercy and of the demand for obedience to His will which His grace lays upon us. When ritual becomes a human performance, an end in itself, with its center on man rather than on God, we must rescue it from the ritualists and transform it into an instrument for God's glory.

The Elements of Worship

In evangelical worship the Word of God is always central. But what is the Word of God? In the Bible, more than mere words, God's Word is His act; and the primary place where He has acted for our salvation is in Jesus Christ. Supremely, Jesus is God's Word. The standard by which we measure worship is the degree to which it confronts men with the Word of Christ, and leads them either to salvation or to judgment.

But how are men confronted by Christ? By reading, preaching, and teaching the Bible. The authority the Bible carries is not an external authority. The Holy Spirit, using the words of Scripture, speaks to us now. The Spirit of God applies the Gospel to our hearts and confronts us with God's redeeming love in Christ.

In his book *Journey into Light,* Emile Cailliet, a Princeton Theological Seminary professor, tells us about his student days and the naturalistic philosophy he found in the European schools. During World War I he spent long night watches in foxholes with a strange longing for "a book that would understand" him.

After a bullet found its mark in his body, and a nine-month stay in a hospital, Cailliet resumed his study. Then one day his bride received a Bible from a French minister. "I literally grabbed the Book and rushed to my study with it," Cailliet said. "I could not find words to express my awe and wonder. And suddenly it dawned upon me! This was the Book that would understand me! . . . I continued to read deeply into the night, mostly from the Gospels. And lo and behold, as I looked through them, the One of whom they spoke, the One who spoke and acted in them, became alive in me" (Grand Rapids: Zondervan, 1968, p. 18).

That is why the church accepts the Bible and makes it central in worship. We read it, preach it, and teach it. Even congregational singing witnesses to its message, and prayers should breathe its atmosphere. The whole service of worship should make real and contemporary the redeeming Word of God.

The most effective way to plant biblical truth in the hearts of men is through preaching. In true preaching, Christ, the living Word of God, makes Himself known through the Scriptures unfolded by the preacher. God Himself speaks through that declaration and offers men His salvation. "Consequently, faith comes from hearing the message, and the message is heard through the word of Christ" (Rom. 10:17, NIV). The sermon, therefore, rather than being a dull speech tolerated by the congregation, should be the heartbeat of worship.

If congregations think of worship in terms of anthems, stained glass, and robed priests, and of preaching as a test of endurance, it is often because the preacher has forgotten the aim of true proclamation. It is to set forth the glory of God in His love and holiness and power. It is to declare the mighty acts of God wrought for people and their salvation. It is to present Jesus Christ as the incarnate, crucified, and exalted Saviour of aimless and powerless people. When that is done, the hearts of hearers are lifted up in gratitude and hope. That is worship.

This is true, of course, only when preachers preach the Christ of Scripture, for only then does the Holy Spirit take the words of the preacher and apply God's Word to the hearts of people. When the Bible is preached, and the Holy Spirit uses the preacher's words, preaching becomes an effective way by which God offers His love to people and calls them to worship.

In addition to the reading of the Scriptures, and the preaching and teaching based on them, Christians have always recognized other elements of worship. The singing of psalms and hymns is a way men respond to God's grace in praise and adoration. The value of singing, whether choral or congregational, does not lie in the quality of the music. It lies in the sincerity and intelligence of the channel of true praise. Singing without clarity of words, therefore, or with words which are sentimental or man-centered rather than a reflection of the glory of God, should be rejected in evangelical worship.

Prayer, too, is a definite part of worship. In prayer the congregation unitedly bows before God. It is man's way of recognizing that all his fountains are in God, that apart from Him man can do nothing. Maxie B. Dunham, in *Channels of Challenge,* quoted someone named Frederick B. Speakman as saying, "The man who has nothing before which he is eager to bow will someday be flattened by the sheer weight of himself." (Nashville: Abingdon Press, 1965, p. 35.)

Prayer is also a means of offering ourselves to God as instruments of His will, as obedient servants whose purpose in life is to strive for those things God wants done in the world.

Most worship services also include an offering. The offering is not an intrusion of secular affairs into worship. It is an opportunity for the worshipers to give concrete expression to their obedient response to God's grace. Do we love God because of His grace? Do we desire His will to be done on earth as it is in heaven? Our answer lies less in what we say than in what we offer.

The Lord's Supper

The supreme element of biblical worship, however, is the celebration of the Lord's Supper. The New Testament makes clear that Jesus intended this special meal to be observed again and again by the church.

Evangelical Christians have often stressed that the Lord's Supper is not a sacrifice offered to God to atone for sin. They know that Christ alone "has once suffered for sins . . . that He might bring us to God" (1 Peter 3:18), and that "we have been sanctified through the offering of the body of Jesus Christ once for all" (Heb. 10:10, RSV). The church, they contend, has no power in the Holy Communion to re-create or to "re-present" the sacrifice of Jesus.

We may grant all this and still miss the meaning of the Lord's Table. What is it? It is a saving message addressed to believers in visible form. What the Gospel is to our ears, the Lord's Supper is to our eyes. It speaks of a past event, a present experience and a future hope.

The past event is the sacrifice of our Lord on Calvary and His triumph at the Tomb. Although we do not want to forget anything else that He did, it is this that was central when He urged, "This do in remembrance of Me" (1 Cor. 11:24). In this event the great friendship was made; God received unholy men. God was in Christ reconciling the world to Himself (2 Cor. 5:19). The believing church accepts anew God's forgiveness as all share in the Lord's Table.

The present experience of the Lord's Supper involves three realities: proclamation, covenant, and communion. Paul told the Corinthians, "as often as you eat this bread and drink the cup, you proclaim the Lord's death" (1 Cor. 11:26, RSV). The Supper is a sermon in action, the Gospel in drama. The assembled church proclaims in a clear fashion the Gospel of God's grace, and Christ is publicly portrayed as crucified.

The Supper is also a covenant. "This cup," said Jesus, "is the New Covenant in My blood" (1 Cor. 11:25, RSV). The Old Covenant was, of course, the unique relationship which God established with Israel during the Exodus and at Mount Sinai. Israel became God's special people by the blood of the sacrificed lamb and the power of His deliverance from the slavery of Egypt.

The Lord's Supper presents a new divine-human relationship, a way which writes no laws upon stones but love upon the heart. "I will put My law within them, and I will write it upon their hearts; and I will be their God, and they shall be My people" (Jer. 31:33, RSV). This is what Jeremiah envisioned but what Jesus established. The church is now God's special people, made His by Christ's blood and the Spirit's power. And the congregation celebrates this grand reality when it observes the Lord's Supper.

Christians have often debated just how God is united with this people in Holy Communion. Those who say Christ is bodily present in the bread and wine go beyond the simple statements of the New Testament and attribute to Paul theological ideas of a later age. In 1 Corinthians 11:23-26 Paul made no simple equation: bread equals body, wine equals blood. Instead of bread and wine, Paul's parallel is bread and cup. The notion of drinking blood would probably have been as repulsive to Paul as to any other Jew. Furthermore, the idea that in eating and drinking the elements he was consuming Christ, somehow really present, would have been equally distasteful.

No, Christ is present in the Supper not in the bread and wine but in His people as they gather to break the bread and drink from the cup. Their symbolic action is not simply a memory device but a way of making the past event of Christ's death present and real for the family of faith. In their meeting together in Gospel memory and expectation, they have communion with Jesus Christ and with one another (1 Cor. 10:16).

Perhaps the greatest abuse of the Supper among evangelicals is the Corinthian abuse—failure to "discern the body." Under the impact of American individualism, many evangelicals have come to think of communion in strictly personal terms. Many pastors contribute to this mood by stressing "let a man examine himself" as they lead in the serving of the elements.

Paul's discussion of the proper conduct of the Table in 1 Corinthians, however, shows clearly that discerning the body means recognizing that the saving events of the Supper—Christ's death, resurrection and coming—are portrayed in the church. The Lord's Supper is supremely a corporate act, a family table, a participating body.

Failure to see this was the Corinthian sin. They turned their backs on the true meaning of the Supper when they failed to act out of love for their Christian brothers. Some began to eat before others arrived. Some gorged themselves while others went hungry (1 Cor. 11:21). Such conduct, said Paul, was scandalous. Drunks at the Lord's Table! And even worse, drunks with a false sense of superiority and an indifference to the needs of brothers in Christ!

According to Paul, to attempt to celebrate the Lord's Supper without recognizing Christ in the midst of His church, binding it together in the love of God, was to eat and drink without discerning the body. "Let a man examine himself" means that the believer must live in the light of Christ's presence with His people. To love Christ is to love His people.

The final evidence that the Lord's Supper is a participation in the Gospel is found in the note of hope. Paul told the Corinthians: "You proclaim the Lord's death until He comes" (1 Cor. 11:26, RSV). The Apostle never thought of Christ's death apart from His resurrection; and resurrection spelled hope.

Some people seek a mood of sadness in the Supper—remembering the Lord's death. Clearly, the observance is no light-hearted affair, but the shout of victory is there. Believers should enter into the gladness and expectation of Christ's return. After all, the early Christians' cry—*Maranatha,* "Our Lord, Come"—is also part of the New Covenant.

The richness of the Gospel message depicted by the Lord's Supper is captured in the words of Mrs. Rundle Charles' hymn:

> No gospel like this feast,
> Spread for Thy Church by Thee;
> Nor prophets nor evangelists
> Preach the glad news more free:
> All our redemption cost,
> All Thy redemption won;
> All it has won for us, the lost,
> All it cost Thee, the Son.

8

The Maturity of the Church

Gettysburg holds a special place in the memory of Americans. The little town in southern Pennsylvania was the site for one of the greatest battles ever fought in the Western Hemisphere. There on July 3, 1863, General Robert E. Lee, hoping to gain foreign recognition for the Confederate states, ordered 15,000 men under General George Pickett to attack the Union Army of the Potomac. Under murderous fire, the men swept across an open field and up the slopes of Cemetery Ridge. A fraction of the men reached the top and for 20 minutes they held their ground. Then, yielding to superior strength, they fell back.

Pickett's charge has often been called "the high-water mark of the Confederacy." It proved to be a turning point. Never again would Lee have the strength to undertake a major offensive. The conflict raged on, but after Gettysburg the outcome of the Civil War was clear.

Christian morality has a similar turning point. The New Testament teaches that the decisive battle in the church's spiritual conflict was fought and won at Calvary. The war isn't over. We still wrestle "against the rulers of the darkness of this world" (Eph. 6:12). But the outcome of the war is already clear. Christ is Victor.

The supreme sign that Christ's future victory already belongs to the church is the resurrection of Jesus from the dead on the first Easter morning. Had the tomb not been empty on that morning there would have been no church. But it was empty and it points beyond itself. Christ is the firstfruit of a harvest to come (1 Cor. 15:20).

Christ's victory over the curse of sin, the power of death, and the grip of Satan remains in this age a hidden sign. God, in His mercy, withholds the open display of His sovereignty so that men may repent and believe. So until the day of Christ's return in glory, the church lives by faith and love and hope. These are the three hallmarks of the resurrection life of Christ in a congregation of God's people.

For centuries, theologians have been calling faith, love, and hope the three theological virtues. The term *virtues* is a bit misleading because it suggests that Christians produce them out of their own moral character. The New Testament, however, always makes clear that they are impossible apart from the grace of God. Christians possess them, to be sure, but faith, love and hope always point beyond themselves to the decisive battle at Calvary and the final victory at the Lord's return. We might be nearer the New Testament teaching if we called them *graces*. But whether virtues or graces, they represent the marks of maturity within the church during this age.

"We always thank God when we pray for you," Paul wrote the Colossians, "because we have heard of your *faith* in Christ Jesus and of the *love* you have for all the saints—the faith and love that spring from the *hope* stored up for you in heaven (Col. 1:3-5, NIV; see also Gal. 5:5-6 and Rom. 5:1-5).

On another occasion, when he was trying to lead the Corinthian church away from the arrogant and schismatic exercise of spiritual gifts, Paul reminded them that prophecies would pass away, tongues would cease, and knowledge would fade away, but *faith, hope,* and *love,* he said, would abide forever (1 Cor. 13: 8-13). Spiritual gifts have only a temporary value, but these three graces point us to things eternal.

In a similar way, Peter, writing to the persecuted saints in Pontus, Galatia, Cappadocia, and Bithynia, reminded them that they were born anew to a living *hope* through the resurrection of Jesus, to an inheritance kept in heaven for those who are guarded through *faith* and who *love* Christ even though they have never seen Him (1 Peter 1:1-9).

Finally, we may recall that when Paul thought of the church at Thessalonica, he thanked God for their *faith* and *love* and *hope* (1 Thes. 1:3). The presence of these three graces in the church, however, did not keep the Apostle from urging the Thessalonians to put on "faith and love as a breastplate and the hope of salvation as a helmet" (1 Thes. 5:8). Apparently, it is possible to have these graces and yet be able to add to them.

As the quotations from the Apostles reveal, the order of the three virtues can vary, depending on the emphasis the inspired writer wants to make. And yet the Thessalonian order—faith and love and hope—is worth noting. Faith looks to the commencement of the Christian life, love to its continuance, and hope to its completion. Put another way—faith looks to the past, to what God has done; love looks to the present, to what God is doing now; and hope to the future, to what God will do. Taken together the three spiritual qualities speak to the moral ideal toward which every church strives, because they witness to the resurrection life of the church between the first coming of Christ and His second.

Faith

Unfortunately, most people in the Western world have been trying for generations to live without faith. For more than three centuries, Western civilization has lived in a split-level universe. The lower floor—the world of science and technology—could demonstrate truth because it could measure it. The upper floor—the world of the spirit—was beyond measurement and so without truth. For modern men, faith lived—if at all—on the upper floor, feeding only on feelings and intuition, not truth.

Today, the promise of the gospel of materialism is the good life. It is supposed to be found in a planned community fully equipped with golfing, swimming, horseback riding and security guards. The salvation of Western materialism is carefree living.

But more and more people are finding materialism—like some suburban oil tycoon—suddenly bankrupt. The emptiness of life without faith usually hits us in some personal tragedy—divorce perhaps, or business scandal, or loss of health. When lives built on empty dreams come smashing to earth and strike the fact of human selfishness, people find that confidence in man's power to control his own world is not enough. Faith in God is foundational. That is what the church teaches.

Christians contend that man's unhappiness is rooted in his feverish attempt to invent a happiness without God. And it will not work! The reason is simple: God made us for Himself.

A fish is designed to live in water. It can't survive anywhere else. Remove it from water and it dies. So man is made to live in God. He is the element our spirits need. Nothing else.

When the church says "faith is essential," it means *faith* in a special sense. Faith is often used in a general way, roughly synonymous with confidence: confidence in God, in our country, or in ourselves. But that is very often an appeal to find something within ourselves, and the Bible warns us about that kind of confidence.

Faith in the Bible has two senses. The first is belief, accepting the doctrines of Christianity as true. Man is a bundle of inner conflicts, all related to his estrangement from God. Jesus Christ is our only Saviour. His death and resurrection are God's invitation to find forgiveness for our sins. The Holy Spirit is our power for a new life. And Christ is coming again to establish justice on the earth. All that seems simple enough—at least for anyone raised in the church. But in point of fact, in our day of relativism, it isn't simple at all; the current idea of truth is "true for you." Truth is what a point of view does for you. It has nothing to do with things as they are in fact.

The church, however, must not say the story about Jesus is true because it helps you to live a better life—as though that is your thing—but another person may choose Confucius, camping, or knitting. According to the Bible, the story of Jesus' life, death, and resurrection is true for all men for all time because God was in those events creating the only way to life for all mankind.

The second sense of biblical faith is trust. Biblical faith not only has a rational element—it is supposed to be true as doctrine—it also has a personal element. It is a relation between God and His people. That is why Christians predict only heartaches for people who seek happiness in things, in the good life, and in carefree living.

Faith, in the biblical sense, is not self-confidence—a sort of life continually puffing "I think I can, I think I can," like "the little train that could." It is more like the bright face of a bride as she says "I do" to the young man she trusts to provide for her future. The Christian faith is a relation between living people and Almighty God.

The church that is growing in Christ must always concentrate on both of these aspects of faith. It must improve its understanding of the truths about God and Christ and the Spirit and salvation and man—all revealed in the Bible. That means Christian education. It means family nurture and doctrinal preaching.

But the life of faith also means applying biblical truths to our marital crises and periods of unemployment and news of cancer. Faith must be more than a nod of agreement in a church service; it must be our walk with God through the shadows. That means pastoral care and a fellowship of prayer and a growing personal conviction that God is near—in our tragedies as well as our triumphs. That is faith.

Christians have often debated what leads a Christian to heaven —good actions or faith alone. Some have said, "Good actions are all that matters." Others have said, "Faith alone is all that counts."

Taken in this simple form, both lead to a sort of nonsense. Heaven can't be bought! And faith is more than some intellectual acceptance of a theory about Jesus.

No, Paul commends the faith that works (1 Thes. 1:3; Gal. 5:6). This is the answer to the faith-and-works debate in a nutshell. Any so-called faith in Christ that does not take into account what He says and commands us to do, is not a faith the Bible recommends for heaven. The realities of the Christian life are invisible—but they offer us no escape from responsible action in this life. Quite the contrary, they energize us to be salt and light in the world.

Love

The second spiritual grace—love—echoes today from countless songwriters and multiplied billions of spinning records. But are they singing about the Christian virtue?

Once I spent a Saturday afternoon at a mountain camp in southern California, listening to a remarkable testimony from a young man named Steve. Of Syrian Jewish parentage, Steve had gone to art school in New York City, where he took his scholarship money and plunged into the drug scene—grass, acid, speed—the whole bit.

"What were you looking for when you started on drugs?"

"I was trying to find some way of eliminating guilt," he told me. "Some great purpose in life where I wouldn't feel guilty."

"What made you think that drugs were the answer?"

"Well, they were touted up to be a key to love and to God and the universe. So I decided to give it a try. It is a lot easier to pop a pill than to get on your knees before God."

Steve plunged into an LSD hell, saw his 17-year-old roommate die after someone passed off on him rat poison for heroin, and had the *Tibetan Book of the Dead* read over him while tripping on acid—all in search of love.

Steve's hunger for happiness could be multiplied a million times over, because the need for love is the most universal of human quests.

We need it from the moment we draw breath. Hospitals have discovered that a maternity ward can have the latest of modern equipment, the finest staff, the most sophisticated medications—but none can produce a thriving infant half as well as the simple diet of mother love.

But what is love? Love must be the most abused word in the English language. We use the same term to describe everything from the highest act of sacrifice to the lowest form of lust.

The Greek language, the language of the New Testament, had four words for love.

The first word was *eros* from which we get our term "erotic." This is passion, and romantic, physical love.

Storgē is the second Greek word. *Storgē* is "affection" because it is used most often of family affection, children for parents and parents for children.

Philia is the third term, a warm word suggesting the "cherishing" of another. It indicates closeness and affection for someone near and dear, as in companionship.

As important as passion, affection, and companionship are, none of them describe Christian love. *Eros, storgē,* and *philia* are all words which express an emotion. They are terms that speak of the heart, an experience that comes unsought, a kind of love that we cannot help especially—it just happens.

The term characteristic of God's love and used to identify the Christian virtue is *agapē. Agapē* love is love that does not simply arise in our hearts. It is not primarily an emotion at all. *Agapē* is an expression of the will, the power to love the unlovely.

It is necessary to make this sharp distinction between love as emotion and love as will, because so much sentimentality has grown up around the term. To many people, Christian love means "treating people nicely." It means liking everybody, overlooking all faults and having a good feeling toward everyone.

The fact that we like some people and not others has very little to do with Christian love. This natural liking is neither a sin nor a virtue—any more than your taste for grapefruit or blue cheese dressing is a sin or virtue.

But, of course, what we do about the liking or disliking can be either a sin or a virtue. If we naturally like a person it may be easier to love him in the Christian sense, that is, to will his good. But when it comes to *agapē,* the rule for all of us is simple. Don't waste time with your likes or dislikes of a person. Just do what is best for the other person.

Presbyterian minister Wesley Baker, in his book *More Than a Man Can Take,* tells about the night a drunk came to his study for help. In the drunk's terms, help meant money for another drink. Baker, however, had other help in mind. He took the man to a hospital. There the man became violent. He struggled, kicked the nurse, and struck the doctor in the face before he was finally restrained, sedated, and committed for treatment. Afterward, Baker half apologized to the staff for the disagreeable scene.

"That's quite all right," the doctor said; "the poor fellow needed our help" (Philadelphia: Westminster, 1966, p. 140).

There is a glimpse of *agapē*. The doctor did not approve of the man's action but he did for him what he needed.

The Bible makes clear throughout that I do not have *agapē* love in my heart. I am driven instead by self-interest and shifting emotions. Love as passion, love as affection, even love as companionship I can know, at least in part, but love as selfless caring I can never fully know until God shows it to me and gives it to me.

But that is the Good News of the Gospel. The God of the Bible is a God who loves patiently, persistently, and sacrificially. For God so loved the world that He gave His only Son so that whoever trusts in Him might not perish but have everlasting life (John 3:16). And having the Son, we have love.

According to the Apostle Paul, love is the supreme Christian virtue. In Colossians 3:14 he called it the bond of perfection, but he made no attempt to define it. In 1 Corinthians 13, the summit of his eloquence, Paul described love as the manifestation of the incarnate life of God. Many have pointed out that if we substitute Christ for *agapē* and change the tenses, we find in the chapter a wonderful description of our Lord's manner of life. "Christ suffered long, and was kind; Christ envied not, vaunted not Himself, was not puffed up, did not behave Himself unseemly, sought not His own, was not provoked, took no account of evil; rejoiced not in unrighteousness, but rejoiced with the truth; bore all things, believed all things, hoped all things, endured all things. Christ never failed."

Now this superlative virtue, according to Paul, is poured into the souls of Christians by the Holy Spirit (Rom. 5:5). And what does this do for the church? The most extensive discussion of love in the life of the church is found in Romans 12. Paul explained in this passage that under the influence of *agapē,* church members find a true affection for fellow believers that suppresses their desire for personal superiority (Rom. 12:10). It makes believers industrious because they recall whom they serve (Rom. 12:11). It fills them with hopefulness, and enables them to endure when things are tough and to persevere in prayer (Rom. 12:12).

Love also produces generous and hospitable believers (Rom. 12:13). It makes them sympathetic to other members' joys and troubles (Rom. 12:15). And it prevents divisions in the church arising from pride (Rom. 12:16).

Hope

The third theological virtue, hope, is subordinate to faith and love but necessary nevertheless to carry faith forward and to make love complete. Cast against the background of our times, biblical hope appears as otherworldly as the other two graces.

Twentieth-century man transplanted the human heart, put Telstar into space, and transported astronauts to the Moon. But he also created the gas chambers of Auschwitz, fought gigantic wars in Europe and Asia, and engaged in the atomic incineration of Hiroshima and Nagasaki.

As a result, some men reveal a misplaced confidence in human skill. They claim that man's ingenuity is the hope of the world. At the same time, other men seem to be hypnotized by the fears of nuclear war. They can only speak in terms of Armageddon. Man simply cannot escape his thoughts of the future, so he gets drunk on unfounded optimism or falls prey to his tormenting fears of the future.

When a person lays aside his newspaper and picks up the Scriptures, he finds neither stupid confidence nor tortured fear. He discovers instead a people standing on tiptoes, leaning and looking into the future—with realism. The churches of New Testament times were fortified by hope.

But what is hope? In our common parlance we use *hope* to mean "wish." A girl may ask her friend, "Are you going out with John?"

"Oh," she says, "I hope so." But it is obvious that she has no firm evidence beyond her wish-filled head. Christian hope, however, is more than mere wishing it were so. Wishing is impatient; it looks for some immediate satisfaction. But Christian hope is willing to wait patiently (Rom. 8:24-25) because it has reason to expect results.

Christian hope is also more than optimism because optimism

is largely subjective. The optimistic person tends to think "I'm OK" and project this satisfaction onto life generally. Christian hope, however, is modest; it looks not to itself but to Someone greater.

Christian hope is so unlike any merely human attitude that the New Testament can say that the non-Christian lives without hope (Eph. 2:12). The non-Christian may have his wishes, he may be optimistic by nature, but he is without hope in the Christian sense if he lives without God.

The confident expectation we meet in the New Testament springs not from an unusual breed of men, but from a special appearance of God. "God was in Christ reconciling the world unto Himself" (2 Cor. 5:19), and on the basis of what God has already done in Christ, the Christian waits with confidence for the day when God will fulfill His promise to come again (Titus 2:13).

At the beginning of World War II, when 200,000 Japanese troops compelled General Douglas MacArthur, commander of the U.S. forces, to withdraw from the Philippine Islands, he promised the discouraged Filipinos and Americans, "I shall return."

In February 1945, troops under MacArthur's command did return to Bataan. They forced the Japanese to surrender and freed the surviving Americans and Filipinos. MacArthur kept his promise to return. Christians are confident Jesus will keep His.

The effect of this hope in the church goes beyond mere survival. Paul, writing to the Christians at Thessalonica, recalled their "endurance inspired by hope" (1 Thes. 1:3, NIV).

It is possible for Christians to become so absorbed in biblical prophecy that they use the Bible to escape from the present. They become so intoxicated with the future that they fail to assume their responsibilities in the present. Interest in prophecy, therefore, isn't necessarily Christian hope; according to Paul, hope enables us not to escape but to endure.

But why? What is the basis for the church's confidence in the future? The basis of Christian hope is not some inside information about future events so much as it is Good News about past events. Christian hope rests on the acts of God in history. It is nourished by what God did at Calvary and Joseph's tomb.

A Christian has confidence in the future primarily because he has a past. The sure foundation for the church is the revelation God has given of His truth, His promises that cannot fail, and His ability to fulfill what He has promised—all secured through the person and work of Jesus Christ. The Christian hope is sustained by an unswerving confidence in the fact that Christ has secured the church's future and that, day by day, all things are being fitted together for good by a loving and sovereign God.

Several years ago I spent part of a morning in a waiting room outside the surgery section of a hospital in Denver. My wife had just been wheeled beyond two swinging doors marked "Surgery." The waiting room was crowded with concerned people.

"This," I thought, "is a replica of life itself." Fear, anxiety, and apprehension were written on faces all around the room—each waiting for some word to come from behind those doors. Occasionally, a surgeon would appear and that question would come out, "How is he, Doc? Is there any hope?" For one family there was no hope. An accident had claimed the life of a husband and father.

But when our doctor came through those doors—still in his green surgery uniform—he had a smile on his face. "No problems," he said. "She is going to be all right!" What a relief! What a surge of thankfulness! Hope sprang up. I had the word of one who had gone through those doors—and had come back and promised, "No problems! It's all right!"

That is the basis of the church's hope—as well as its faith and love. Jesus has been on the other side and He has returned to tell us, "It's all right!"

9

The Ministry of
the Church

Bud Wilkinson, former football coach at the University of Oklahoma, was in Dallas some years ago for a series of lectures on physical fitness. A TV reporter interviewed him about the President's physical fitness program and asked: "Mr. Wilkinson, what would you say is the contribution of modern football to physical fitness?" The reporter expected a lengthy speech.

As if he had been waiting 30 years for this question, Wilkinson said, "Absolutely nothing."

The young reporter stared and squirmed and finally stuttered, "Would you care to elaborate on that?"

Wilkinson said, "Certainly. I define football as 22 men on the field who desperately need rest and 50,000 people in the grandstand who desperately need exercise."

That interview strikes at the heart of the problem the church often faces in doing the work of God. It is a twofold dilemma: we suffer from high expectations of the few and we see the low participation of the many.

This is the day of the specialist. I found this out the hard way recently. It began with an intense pain in my back and under my right rib cage. It grew so bad one night that I was rushed to the emergency section of the hospital. After five days in the hospital, my doctor told me to see an internist. I did. My internist told me to see a gastrointestinal specialist. I did. My radiologist told my gastrointestinal specialist I should see a surgeon. I did. My surgeon removed about 50 stones from my body with the assistance of an anesthesiologist.

Name any field and you will find the same thing. Football itself has become so specialized we no longer see the wide receiver or one of the other regular players doing the kicking. No, one man does the punting, another kicks off and a third man kicks the field goals.

In this kind of world, it is only natural that we should look to the specialist to do the work of the Lord. *Call the expert* in Christian circles means, "Let the minister do it." We expect our minister to be:

> an effective speaker
> a sympathetic counselor
> a successful administrator
> a zealous evangelist
> an entertaining host
> an influential social worker
> and a model husband and father.

At the same time, we have turned Christian work into a spectator sport. The limit of the average church member's involvement is about the same as the average football fan's. He does a lot of screaming about how the game ought to be played but he contributes nothing beyond his criticism.

Again, the attitude is understandable—if not excusable—given our social attitudes. We send our children to school to get an education. That's why we pay our taxes. We send our aged mother-in-law to a state hospital for treatment. That's why we pay our taxes. We find the neighbor's dog in our garden, and we call the dogcatcher. That's why we pay our taxes.

We go to church and hear that the high schoolers don't seem to know what to do with themselves when they get together. We vote to hire a youth director. That's why we pay our tithes. Why not? It's the thing to do.

It is the thing to do in the world, but it is producing Christians by proxy in the church. And God never designed Christian service to be contracted out to experts. Because the ministry belongs to the whole church.

The Christian Ministry

The Christian understanding of ministry arises from one primary source, the life and mission of Jesus Christ. Our Lord saw His purpose in the world in terms of service. "The Son of Man," He said, "came not to be ministered unto but to minister and to give His life a ransom for many" (Mark 10:45).

In that unique sense of surrendering His life for our salvation, Jesus has no successors. He is the only ransom available. But in a broader sense of sharing the Gospel and building the church, Jesus made it clear that His followers were to be ministers or servants. Once, He contrasted His disciples to rulers in the world who lord over their subjects. "But it shall not be so among you," He said. "Whosoever will be great among you, let him be your minister (*diakonos,* servant); and whosoever will be chief among you, let him be your servant (*doulos,* slave)" (Matt. 20:26-27).

This ministry, which the Lord's disciples shared, was described in the New Testament as a "ministry of the Word" (Acts 6:4), "a ministry of reconciliation" (2 Cor. 5:18), and "a ministry of the New Covenant" (2 Cor. 3:6). In short, the ministry is almost any effort we make to advance the Gospel, to apply to the hearts of men the unique ministry of Jesus Christ. The servanthood of Jesus led to the cross; the servanthood of the church leads from the cross. That is why Peter could remind the elders that Christ is the chief Shepherd or Pastor (1 Peter 5:4). Other pastors are simply following the Lord's lead in the ministry of reconciliation.

The term most often used to describe Christian service is *diakonia,* from which we get our word "deacon." It suggests common or menial labor. It is service without dignity or status.

Unfortunately *minister* has become one of those terms that suggests office or status in the community. It usually designates an educated religious leader, a professional figure in society. And that dulls the impact of the New Testament idea, for *ministry* in the apostolic writings means labor for Christ without regard to religious rank. It is the privilege and the calling of all the saints.

In this fundamental sense of ministry, the New Testament recognizes no clergy-laity distinction. All ministers are laymen—God's people—and all laymen are ministers.

The words "clergy" and "laity" come from the Greek *kleros* (lot) and *laos* (people). In the Bible, God's *kleros,* the lot that falls to Him as His special possession, is the whole people of God, not a small portion of them in leadership positions. And the *laos,* the people of God, is also the whole company of the Lord's chosen. So in this fundamental sense, all of God's people are ministers. The old idea of a special priesthood to intercede for the people is a thing of the past. After the ministry of Jesus, His sinless life and His atoning death, no priestly class is needed. There is nothing else for a priest to offer God for the sins of men. Jesus paid it all.

Because of special problems in the Corinthian church, the Apostle Paul laid down the principles for the church's ministry in his first letter to that congregation. The Corinthians got carried away by their zeal for spiritual highs. They tried to outdo each other in displaying their spirituality. So Paul had to write to them, explaining the nature and purpose of the Spirit's gifts.

The Gifts of the Spirit

Paul makes several important points in 1 Corinthians 12, but consider three of the major ones.

First, he taught that every believer shares in the gifts from the Holy Spirit. Each has a "manifestation of the Spirit" (1 Cor. 12:7, RSV). If we continued our football analogy, we would have to say that a winning team demands that every player make his contribution.

Professional football has become so expensive, salaries are so high, that every player has to be able to contribute. That means he has to be physically fit and able to do his job.

In a similar way, Paul argued that every church member is equipped by God to serve. No one can say, "Jesus is Lord," except by the Holy Spirit. Every believer is given the Holy Spirit. He is the Christian's new life, his life "in Christ" (1 Cor. 12:3). And we know that the Holy Spirit has come to witness to Jesus Christ

(John 16:13-14). Just as our body moves and thinks and runs and works as it is animated by an invisible power within us—called life—so the church and every member in it is moved by the Holy Spirit.

So the Christian ministry—our service for Jesus Christ—is simply an extension of the confession of faith we make when we say, "Jesus is Lord."

This ministry has two dimensions. When we direct our service outside the church it is evangelism. It is making Christ known to those who do not know Him, by what we do and say and are. In Ephesians 4, another passage discussing spiritual gifts, Paul tells us that evangelists are given to the church for the "equipment of the saints, for the work of ministry" (Eph. 4:11-12). When we direct our service inside the church, it is edification. It is strengthening one another in faith and love and hope until the church reflects the desires and likeness of its head, Jesus Christ.

This ministry is as varied as the members of a human body. And all the members are needed. Paul stressed that when he wrote, "If the whole body were an eye, where would the sense of hearing be?" (1 Cor. 12:17, NIV) Eyes are beautiful members, but how would we function if we were just one 150-pound blue eye? One member simply cannot serve alone. God has given each member to the body so that the diversity of youth and age, zeal and wisdom, abundance and need might work together under the coordinating control of the Head of the body, the Lord Jesus Christ.

My eye does a great job in spotting an orange, but if the orange is to nourish me, my eye is not enough. My hand grasps it, my fingers peel it, my mouth encloses a piece, my teeth chew it, my tongue moves it around properly, my throat swallows it, my stomach digests it—the list could be extended almost *ad infinitum*. Every member serves. That is the point.

In his book *The Company of the Committed,* Elton Trueblood makes an observation that many of us have found true. "As we consider what has been crucial in our lives," he writes, "we become aware of the fact that most of the testimonies which have helped us have been virtually unconscious ones. . . . This is as it should be. In a group of twenty-five lay Christians meeting recently, each told what was the major influence which had helped him to move over from nominal Christianity to a committed faith. Every one of the twenty-five mentioned a *person*. Not one mentioned a public occasion. And the surprising part was that all of the persons mentioned as thus effective in personal ministry were inconspicuous. Most of them had made a significant witness without knowing it" (*The Company of the Committed*, New York: Harper and Row, 1961, p. 64).

For years, I have been impressed with the response of those who will be commended when the Son of Man comes to sit on His glorious throne. The sheep will be separated from the goats. And the King will say to some, "Come, inherit the kingdom prepared for you . . . for I was hungry and you gave Me food, . . . I was naked and you clothed Me, I was sick and you visited Me." Then the righteous will answer, "When did we see Thee hungry, when did we see Thee naked, when did we see Thee sick?" (Matt. 25:31-46) The righteous are unaware of their service to Christ, because they serve hungry and naked and sick people just because they need help, not in order to gain a reward.

With all of the emphasis on spiritual gifts in recent years, we may need that reminder that true service is seldom conscious of the exercise of some gift or even the idea of service. Love is not arrogant; it is kind.

The Unity of the Gifts
Second, Paul teaches that the various gifts, given to church members, are nevertheless united in the one ministry unto Jesus Christ. Or if we make the same point in terms of football, we'd say a winning team works together as a single unit.

A football player can be a perfect specimen of manhood on the gridiron. He can weigh 255 pounds, run the 40-yard dash in 4.5 seconds, bench press twice his weight and flatten a runner like a freight train. And still not make the team—if he never learns to blend his talents with the whole squad.

If it is true in athletics, it is equally true in the ministry for Christ. Christianity is not made for superstars who never learn to work with others in the body. Gifts of the Spirit cannot be exercised alone; they are given to the church for the growth of the church.

The Corinthians had not learned that lesson. Paul's remarks in the twelfth chapter of his first letter reveal two equally damaging attitudes in the church.

The first attitude said, "I don't belong." Paul wrote, "If the foot should say, 'Because I am not a hand, I do not belong to the body,' it would not for that reason cease to be part of the body. And if the ear should say, 'Because I am not an eye, I do not belong to the body,' it would not for that reason cease to be part of the body."

Why wouldn't it? Because, as Paul wrote, God has arranged the parts in the body, every one of them just as He wanted them to be (1 Cor. 12:14-20).

Like some mosquito bite, Paul's argument gets under our skin. Which of us hasn't said at some time, "I don't belong." We may have said it when we have been hurt. No one appreciated us. No one mentioned how many hours we put into planning that reception. No one realized how long we spent phoning people for the nursery. "I guess I don't really belong to this church."

But we do belong. Men didn't arrange the parts in the body. God did. And the hurt we feel may be the voice of God trying to get through to us. He may be trying to teach us something about true service, service not for our reputation but for His.

The second attitude said, "I don't need you!" Paul wrote, "The eye cannot say to the hand, 'I don't need you!' "

Why can't the eye say that? Because God has combined the members of the body and has given greater honor to the parts that lack it, so that there should be no division in the body (1 Cor. 12:21-26).

But what happens when there is disagreement? When points of difference do come up, each member should consider the well-being of the others.

In my own body, for example, there is a disagreement. My palate loves cucumbers but my stomach does not. The solution? I've given up cucumbers! Or, if I have an infection in my lung, my arm (which is not at all infected) is glad to bear the pain of the injection of antibiotics in order to protect another member of the body. That is what God has in mind for the church. "Outdo one another," the Apostle wrote, "in showing honor" (Rom. 12:10, RSV).

The Goal of the Gifts

Third, Paul taught that the goal of these gifts is not our personal reputation but a mature body. In terms of football, we would have to say that the goal that motivates a player to keep running, to lift weights, and to control his diet is the championship. The goal that keeps an offensive unit practicing every step, every move, every minute detail—over and over and over again—is the pride and prestige of being champions.

In a similar way, the thing that keeps a church striving for improvement, developing leadership, teaching the young, and helping the weak is the vision of the goal. In 1 Corinthians 12:7 Paul called it simply "the common good" (RSV). But in Ephesians 4:13 he called it "the full measure of perfection found in Christ" (NIV).

But what does that mean? What is a winning church? When champions are crowned in Christian ministry what do they look like? Well, they somehow look like Christ; they have grown up to their Head, as Paul put it in Ephesians 4:15. But can we be more specific? In the Ephesians 4 passage, especially verses 14-16, we find three characteristics of a mature church.

First, it is steadfast in the truth. Paul compared it to a stable vessel at sea "no longer . . . tossed back and forth by the waves, and blown here and there by every wind of teaching" (Eph. 4:14, NIV).

The mature church knows the Gospel—the sinfulness of man, the grace of God, the atoning sacrifice of Jesus, His bodily resurrection from the dead, the gift of the Holy Spirit, and the confident hope of the Lord's return. The mature church knows this and is not swayed by religious fads, personality cults or false teaching.

Second, the mature church is united in Christ. "From Christ," says Paul, "the whole body is joined and held together" (Eph. 4:16). Individual gifts and prejudices and opinions do not destroy the oneness of the new life in Christ. Mature churches learn to face differences without those convictions fracturing the fellowship of the Spirit.

Third, the mature church grows in love. Paul put it this way, "the whole body . . . grows and builds itself up in love, as each part does its work" (Eph. 4:16, NIV). So the goal of the ministry is a loving community where each person makes his gifts count either in winning those outside or building up those on the inside.

In the New Testament, the ministry of the church is reduced to member helping member and the whole church bearing witness and service to others in the name of Christ.

Dag Hammarskjold, the former Secretary-General of the United Nations, once wrote, "The 'great' commitment all too easily obscures the 'little' one. But without the humility and warmth which you have to develop in your relations to the few with whom you are personally involved, you will never be able to do anything for the many" (*Markings,* New York: Alfred A. Knopf, 1972, p. 133). I think he was right.

10

Leadership in the Church

In John Bunyan's *Pilgrim's Progress,* Christian came in the course of his journey to the House of the Interpreter. He was taken into a private room, where he saw "the picture of a very grave person hanging up against the wall; and this was the fashion of it: it had eyes lifted up to heaven, the best of books in his hand, the law of truth was written upon his lips, the world was behind its back; it stood as if it pleaded with men, and a crown of gold did hang over its head."

This is Bunyan's portrait of the evangelical preacher. Every feature of it is instructive. But for our purposes, the most significant are the words, "the best of books in his hand." According to Bunyan, the Gospel minister has a firm grasp of the truth—the truth of God revealed in Holy Scripture; and that truth of God is not only in his hand but also on his lips: "He stood as if he pleaded with men."

The image of the Christian minister has changed greatly since the 1660s, but the ministerial leadership remains the same—the man of God with the Word of God before the people of God.

Gifts for Spiritual Leadership
The spiritual gifts given by the Holy Spirit to every member for ministry in the body do not negate the necessity of spiritual

leadership in the church. The New Testament speaks of leaders in the church as "those over you in the Lord" (1 Thes. 5:12, RSV). It is clear that the local church functions best when the ones who are weak in the faith find the support of spiritual leaders (Gal. 6:1).

At first glance, however, the New Testament seems disturbingly indecisive about the specific kind of government God had in mind for His church. The primary interest of the New Testament literature is in the life and mission of the church, not in its leadership. It seems that the Spirit of God has allowed a certain flexibility in the names and duties of the officials. That helps to explain the persistent differences among Christian denominations. Some have elders, others have bishops, and still others have pastors to lead the church.

Furthermore, the freedom to exercise the gifts of prophecy in the apostolic churches and the special office of an Apostle make direct parallels with today's churches more than a little risky.

The simple fact is that no specific church government is legislated in the New Testament. That means that boasting about a superior polity (church government) is suspect from the start. Richard Hooker, the 16th-century Anglican churchman, recognized the clearer and weightier matters of faith and love and hope. In his *Laws of Ecclesiastical Polity* he wrote, "Happier are they whom the Lord when He cometh, shall find doing these things, than disputing about 'doctors, elders, and deacons.' "

At the same time the New Testament does make clear that the ministry of the Word requires that the affairs of the church be conducted decently and in an orderly fashion. Paul, for example, was quite clear. His primary concern was with the spiritual realities rather than the details of outward form, but church order must be maintained if faith and love and hope are to flourish.

Two factors seem to have contributed to the way early Christians thought of leadership. First was tradition; second was the Spirit.

When the church emerged in Jerusalem, it drew upon existing Jewish institutions. Since most—if not all—of the earliest believers were Jews, they were accustomed to the mode of government that prevailed in the synagogue. The office of elder, for example, came into Christianity quite naturally.

The New Testament teaching regarding spiritual gifts offers another primary explanation of the place of spiritual leadership in the church. In Ephesians, chapter 4, Paul taught that the ascended Christ gave gifts of grace to every member (Eph. 4:7-8). But among these gifts to the church were apostles, prophets, evangelists and pastor-teachers (Eph. 4:11).

The first two—apostles and prophets—were given by the Lord at the beginning of the church to serve as the foundation for the building in the years that followed (Eph. 2:20). Apostles and prophets were especially important as instruments of revelation. They received the Word of God and delivered it to the church for all generations. The "foundation" figure suggests that other teachers can build on the message of the apostles and prophets but they cannot change it.

Evangelists have a continuing ministry in the church as leaders in spreading the saving knowledge of Christ to those without a personal experience of God's grace. Since those without Christ are primarily in the world, the evangelist serves the church best by going to the world with his message of God's forgiveness and grace.

Finally, the Apostle mentioned "pastors and teachers" (Eph. 4:11). The two gifts are joined in such a way that we know Paul is thinking of one group of leaders who shepherd and teach. That can only mean the spiritual leaders in the local churches.

Pastors and Teachers

The New Testament speaks often of the essentials of this leadership in the local church. In Acts 20, we read of Paul's invitation to the Ephesian elders to meet him at Miletus where he reviewed his ministry among them and charged them with the spiritual oversight of the church at Ephesus. "Be on guard for yourselves," he told them, "and for all the flock, among which the Holy Spirit has made you overseers, to shepherd the church of God, which He purchased with His own blood" (Acts 20:28, NASB).

This important verse tells us several things about leadership in the early local churches. First, these men served by divine appointment. It was the Spirit who made them *overseers* or *shepherds*. While the church shares in the recognition of the gifts for the ministry of the Word—in a service we call *ordination*—a minister of the Gospel must always sense the hand of God in his selection for service. There is something supernatural in his call. "No man," says the Epistle to the Hebrews, "takes this honor upon himself; he must be called by God, just as Aaron was" (Heb. 5:4, NIV).

Second, Acts 20:28 indicates that the spiritual leaders in the church were called *elders* or *overseers* (bishops) or *pastors* (shepherds). The same position could be designated by any of the terms.

Probably the most revealing designation of a minister of the Gospel is *shepherd* (or pastor) because the picture of the shepherd and his sheep is deeply woven into the language and imagery of the Bible. The reason is simple. The main part of Judea is a central plateau. It stretches from Bethel to Hebron for a distance of 35 miles. The ground, for the most part, is rough and stony, better for grazing of sheep than for raising of crops. So the most familiar figure to be seen on the Judean highlands became the shepherd.

Travelers in Palestine tell us that shepherds may still be found leaning on their staffs looking after their scattered sheep. Once you see these farsighted, weather-beaten watchmen, you can understand why the shepherd of Judea was so popular in his people's history, why he gave his name to their King and why Jesus took him as the example of self-sacrifice (John 10:1-18).

The Old Testament often pictures God as the Shepherd and the people of Israel as His flock. The psalmists were especially fond of this figure: "The Lord is my Shepherd," we read, "I shall not want" (Ps. 23:1). "We Thy people and sheep of Thy pasture will give Thee thanks forever" (Ps. 79:13, RSV). And "We are His people, and the sheep of His pasture" (Ps. 100:3, RSV).

God's Anointed One, the Messiah, was also pictured as the Shepherd of the sheep. "He shall feed His flock like a shepherd," wrote Isaiah. "He shall gather the lambs with His arm, and carry them in His bosom, and shall gently lead those that are with young" (Isa. 40:11).

The leaders of the people are also described as the shepherds of God's people and nation. "Woe be unto the pastors that destroy and scatter the sheep of My pasture" (Jer. 23:1). Ezekiel had a tremendous indictment of the false leaders who sought their own good rather than the good of the flock. "Woe be unto the shepherds of Israel that do feed themselves! Should not the shepherds feed the flock?" (Ezek. 34:2)

This picture passes over into the New Testament, where Jesus is the Good Shepherd. Jesus likened Himself to the shepherd who sought at the peril of his life for the one sheep that had gone astray (Matt. 18:12-14; Luke 15:4-7). He sent out His disciples to gather in the lost sheep of the house of Israel (Matt. 10:6). He was moved with pity for the crowds, for they were as sheep without a shepherd (Matt. 9:36; Mark 6:34). And, above all, Jesus described Himself as the Good Shepherd who was ready to lay down His life for the sheep (John 10:11).

Thus, when Peter and Paul referred to church leaders as pastors (or shepherds), they were placing ministers in a noble heritage. It suggests that the attitude of the elder to the flock, the church, must be the same as God's attitude to His people.

What a vision opens out! What an ideal! The minister of the Gospel must show to people the forbearance of God, the forgiveness of God, the seeking love of God, the illimitable service of God. God has assigned to him a task and he must do it as God Himself would do it. That is the supreme ideal of service in the Christian church.

Responsibilities of a Pastor

As the Acts 20:28 text shows, the responsibilities of the spiritual leaders in a congregation fall into three primary areas.

The pastor-elder's first responsibility is *to be an example* for the flock. This note is struck in almost every passage dealing with leadership in the church. In his first letter, Peter wrote, "To the elders among you, I appeal as a fellow elder. . . . Be shepherds of God's flock that is under your care, serving as overseers . . . but being examples to the flock" (1 Peter 5:1-3, NIV).

In a similar way, where the Apostle Paul discussed the standards for an overseer, the example of a pastor's life was paramount: in the use of money, in the management of his family, in the control of his temperament, and in his reputation before "outsiders" (1 Tim. 3:1-7).

The New Testament assumes throughout that the church needs the stimulus, the encouragement, and the direction of a spiritual model, from the Chief Shepherd of the church, first of all, but also from "under shepherds." Mark Twain put it pungently in his *Pudd'nhead Wilson* when he said, "Few things are harder to put up with than the annoyance of a good example."

The pastor-elder's second responsibility is *to oversee* the flock. "Take heed unto yourselves," Paul told the Ephesian elders, "and to all the flock" (Acts 20:28, RSV). And we know what he had in mind. He told them to beware of men who "distort the truth" (Acts 20:30, NIV). Identifying error and counteracting it is an ever-present obligation of a pastoral leader. Next, Paul warned the leaders of the Ephesian church about factions in the fellowship, men who "draw away disciples after them" (Acts 20:30, NIV). The shepherd's concern must always be the safety and unity of the flock. And finally, the passage makes clear that oversight includes helping the weak even, if necessary, with material needs (Acts 20:35). The shepherd never looks after souls alone; he cares for sheep.

This kind of oversight of the flock demands that a shepherd know his sheep. He must go with them through life's shadows and over rough paths. In our impersonal metropolitan communities, that may be difficult, but there is no substitute for this identity with the people of God, knowing their needs, feeling their pains, and sensing their aspirations. Peter T. Forsyth, who had so many striking things to say about the ministry, once wrote, "You must live with people to know their problems, and live with God in order to solve them" (*Cure of Souls*, p. 27).

The pastor-elder's third responsibility is *to feed* the flock. "Take heed," Paul told the Ephesian leaders, "to feed the church of God" (Acts 20:28). That involves what the New Testament calls the "labor of preaching and teaching" the Word of God (1 Tim. 5:17, RSV). In our day, that means he must be a lifelong student of the Bible and the skills necessary to communicate it effectively to his people.

In this regard, I have always liked the old distinction that I first learned from Halford E. Luccock, the well-known Methodist preacher. Preaching, he said, should be a sector of the truth and not an arc. An arc is a portion of the circumference of a circle; a sector is a V-shaped wedge in a circle, which includes a portion of the circumference but goes by radii to the center.

Arc preaching deals with a segment of the circumference of life. It is contemporary, topical, and relevant, but it does not touch the center. It is preaching in the tradition of the oft-quoted remark of Arnold Lunn: "There is no market for sermons on the text: God so loved the world that He inspired a certain Jew to inform His contemporaries that there was a great deal to be said for loving one's neighbors." Jesus Christ's mission involved more than that. If He was not born to save us from our sins, then our preaching is in vain.

Sector preaching, on the other hand, includes the circumference but it goes to the center. It cuts to the heart of the Gospel and lifts out the grace of God for all to see (Halford E. Luccock, *In the Minister's Workshop,* Nashville: Abingdon, 1944, pp. 38-40).

The ideal of the shepherding ministry is extremely rare today. This is due, in part, to the fact that the pastoral role in the twentieth century has become unbelievably complex. Congregations are often much larger and more scattered. Three hospital calls in many cities may require an afternoon of travel and counsel. Church organizations are complicated with multiplied boards, committees, and budgets. The pressure is always on a minister of the Gospel to become an administrator of the program. Study time and spiritual reflection often get crowded out, so the New Testament model for ministry, preacher of the Word and physician of souls, often seems like a long lost ideal.

Yet pastoral leadership remains essentially the same today as in New Testament times because the needs of men and the nature

of the church remain the same. Many churches need to understand this and to encourage their ministers to return to the basics
of biblical ministry.

Deacons

One of the ways pastor-teachers can return to their biblical calling
is suggested by the action of the early church when faced with
the same problem. We read in Acts 6 that a dispute arose among
the Grecian Jews in the Jerusalem church. They felt their widows
were being neglected in the welfare program of the church. In
order to solve the problem, the Apostles urged the church to
select seven men to oversee the program so that the Twelve
could continue to give their attention to "prayer and the ministry
of the Word" (Acts 6:4, RSV). The church accepted the proposal.
Seven men were chosen and "the Word of God spread" (Acts
6:7, RSV). The Apostles had a clear vision of divine priorities.
Topping the list was the "ministry of the Word." Preaching and
teaching should remain a priority.

The selection of the seven men, "of honest report, full of the
Holy Ghost and wisdom," to assume the duties of distributing to
the needs of widows so that the Apostles could give their attention to the ministry of the Word, probably marks the institution of the office of deacon. The title was not used of the seven
men chosen. But we know from the First Letter to Timothy,
where Paul gave clear directions for the selection of deacons,
that they joined the overseers or pastors in the leadership of the
early churches (1 Tim. 3:8-13). The New Testament clearly
supports the idea of a shared ministry. Deacons are a reminder of
that concept.

The work of the deacons in the early church is not entirely
clear. Apparently, they had responsibility for the administration
of funds and particularly the distribution of relief to the poor
members of the church. We should not insist, however, upon a
timeless "job description" for the office in the hopes of following
it slavishly. It is enough to be clear on the fact that deacons
should assist in the affairs of the church so as to free pastor-
elders for the "ministry of the Word." Paul indicated in 1 Timothy

3:8-13 that, in order to do this, deacons should possess spiritual maturity, trustworthiness, and administrative ability.

Ordination
Some churches ordain their deacons but many reserve ordination for pastors or other ministers called to a lifetime service. Missionaries, military chaplains and theological professors would be examples of the extension of the pastoral role. In any case, ordained leadership is to an office, not to a status. The ordination of a man to the ministry does not give him special powers unavailable to his fellow Christians. Ordination is simply the church's formal recognition of a divine call to special spiritual leadership in the church and of the gifts needed for the fulfillment of that call.

Men are ordained to preach and teach within the church not because they are the most committed, but because they have been given certain gifts of leadership to be used to help God's people (equally committed) to fulfill their work in His service "to the building up of the body of Christ" (Eph. 4:11-13, NASB). As long as an ordained man feels (even unconsciously) that his theological education and ordination are signs of a will more given to God than that of a committed lawyer or housewife, then that pastor will think of his role as the true role of commitment. He must resist the temptation to shape his people into his own image. His true calling is to help them to become the creative businessmen and parents and housewives they were gifted by God to be.

Beyond this, the pastor-teacher must live in the world along with all the other members of the church. He is a citizen, probably a husband and father, and has other roles as well. In these worldly relationships, the clergyman ought to function as a layman, for nothing in his ordination prepares him for any privileged role in the world. His ordained functions are in the church. In the world he is a member of the body of Christ along with all other laymen.

11

The Mission of the Church

The human family is divided into two groups. Not just male and female or rich and poor. The most basic distinction in human society, from the Christian perspective, is church and world.

This difference is not the result of an arbitrary decision made by Christians—as though the church were somehow superior to the world. The distinction was made first by Jesus Christ. Our Lord looked below the surface of human behavior and emotions and identified all mankind according to a relationship to God.

As Jesus approached His arrest, trial, and death He warned His disciples that they could expect opposition from the world. "If you belonged to the world," He said, "it would love you as its own. As it is, you do not belong to the world, but I have chosen you out of the world" (John 15:19, NIV). He called His disciples out of the world in order to send them to the world with the Gospel of God's forgiving love.

The fundamental difference between church and world is the knowledge of salvation. "Now this is eternal life," Jesus prayed, "that men may know You, the only true God and Jesus Christ, whom You have sent" (John 17:3, NIV). This exclusive, ultimate relationship not only links a Christian to God; it cuts him off from the world.

In the Bible, the *world* often means the created world—butterflies, pines, and mountains. But the world distinguished from the church, and to which the church is sent with the Gospel, is the world of men who do not know God.

The church always stands in a dual relationship to this world. Jesus summarized it best in John 17 when He spoke of His disciples—"not of the world" but "sent into the world" (John 17:16, 18, NIV). In God's plan, the church feels the rhythm of detachment and involvement, withdrawal and engagement.

This means that the mission of the church must advance to this beat: separation from the world yet penetration of the world. This spells struggle because a Christian must be enough in touch with the world to speak to its needs without being so much like the world that he has nothing to say. Evangelical Christians often differ over the boundaries of engagement and withdrawal.

Not long ago, a well-known evangelist criticized a popular Christian entertainer for accepting appointments in nightclubs known for their sex symbols. The entertainer defended his actions by pointing to the opportunities for witness. Compromise with the world for one Christian was witness to the world for another. The debate is as old as the second century when Tertullian, the North African lawyer, and Clement, the Alexandrian professor, took different positions on the value of Greek philosophy for Christianity.

All Christians agree, however, that the church is sent. That is where we get the idea *mission*. It started with God Himself. He sent His prophets, His Son, and His Spirit. Of these missions, the mission of the Son is central, for it was the culmination of the ministry of the prophets, and it embraced within itself as its climax the sending of the Spirit. During His public ministry, Jesus sent out first the Apostles and then the 70 as a kind of extension of His own preaching, teaching, and healing ministry. After His death and resurrection He widened the scope of the mission to include the whole church.

Evangelism

Until recent years, Christians have nearly always believed that the central mission of the church was evangelism. The rise of liberal ideas, however, including *dialogue* and *liberation,* compel us to emphasize again that the mission of the church centers in a message. More than 2.7 billion people, which is two-thirds of mankind, have yet to hear a meaningful presentation of God's Good News. But nothing hinders evangelism today more than the widespread loss of confidence in the truth and power of the Gospel. When this ceases to be Good News from God and becomes, instead, man's opinion about God, we can hardly expect the church to exhibit much enthusiasm for preaching and teaching the Gospel.

Elton Trueblood, in his book *Incendiary Fellowship,* compared evangelism to a fire. Evangelism occurs, he said, when people are so enkindled by contact with the central fire of Christ that they, in turn, set others on fire. We know that something is on fire by a pragmatic test. Other fires are started by it. A fire that does not spread must eventually go out! (Harper and Row, 1967, p. 111) Christianity without a mission, like fire that does not burn, is a contradiction in terms.

The church faces not only a lack of zeal. It also encounters a misunderstanding of the message. Many people today, within the churches as well as without, don't have the foggiest idea about the evangelistic message.

What is the New Testament Gospel? The Lausanne Covenant, signed by 2,400 evangelicals in 1974, describes it as "The Good News that Jesus Christ died for our sins and was raised from the dead according to the Scriptures, and that as the reigning Lord He now offers the forgiveness of sins and the liberating gift of the Spirit to all who repent and believe."

It is true that the New Testament reflects no rigid stereotype. There are different emphases arising from the authors' backgrounds and temperaments. The Apostle Paul could even speak of "my Gospel" when he mentioned the particular "mystery" God disclosed to him (Rom. 2:16; 2 Tim. 2:8). Furthermore, his sermon in a Jewish synagogue at Antioch diverges sharply from his Areopagus address in Athens. When we allow for all these variations in the New Testament, however, there remains one basic apostolic Gospel. Paul told the Galatians that the Jerusalem

Apostles gave to him "the right hand of fellowship" as a sign of their acknowledgement of his mission and message (Gal. 2:9). And in the same chapters he insisted that there is no other Gospel.

Recent years have presented a threat to this New Testament Gospel. Some have argued that the apostolic message cannot be for our age because it was shaped by culture. It is true that in God's plan, His revelation culminated during the first century A.D., in Christ and the apostolic witness. It was an ancient culture, blending Hebrew, Greek, and Roman elements. So in order to grasp this revelation, we have to think ourselves back into that culture. But the fact that God disclosed Himself in a particular culture is no reason to reject the revelation. We have the responsibility to reinterpret it in terms that people in our own culture can understand. But there is only one Gospel, and in its essence it never changes.

Preaching the Gospel always demands two things. Bishop Phillips Brooks of Boston once called them "truth and timeliness." Our message must be both faithful and contemporary. We find our message not in a current need but in the Bible.

We can never describe true evangelism as answering the questions men are asking. The Bible teaches that evangelism is first and above all the communication of God's question to man. That crucial question was, and is to this day, whether we accept Jesus Christ as the one and only Lord of Life.

As English clergyman John Stott has written, "It is comparatively easy to be faithful if we do not care about being contemporary, and easy also to be contemporary if we do not bother to be faithful. It is the search for a combination of truth and relevance which is exacting. Yet nothing else can save us from an insensitive loyalty to formulae and shibboleths on the one hand, and from a treasonable disloyalty to the revelation of God on the other" (*Christian Mission,* Downer's Grove: InterVarsity Press, 1975, p. 43).

Social Concern

This concern to apply the Gospel to man's need today has led many evangelical Christians to ask about the relation between evangelism and social responsibility. The Christian lives in the world as well as in the church, and has responsibilities to the world as well as to the church. Unfortunately, churches tend to "ecclesiasticize" their members. Their obedience to Christ runs only in institutional or pietistic channels: meetings and programs, or prayer meetings and discipleship groups.

Our evangelism often takes the convert out of the world and never sends him back into it. Our goal must be the mission of the same person in the same world, and yet a new person with new convictions and new standards. If Jesus' first command was "Come," His second was "Go." We must reenter the world out of which we have come, only now as Christ's ambassadors.

But how? What is the relation between membership in the church and witness in the world? There are three possibilities. We may preach the Gospel without any sight of its social context. Or we may preach a social gospel which omits the necessity of conversion to Christ. Or we may preach the Gospel, making it clear that it is the whole man with all his relationships who is converted to Jesus as the Lord of all he is and does.

If we recognize the third obligation—as numbers of evangelical Christians do—how can a church express its social responsibility? Terms are important here, so let me offer three definitions: social concern, social welfare, and social action.

Social concern is an attitude. It is the Christian awareness that salvation is directed to the whole man. It is a recognition of the Gospel's application to the hurts and hungers of man as well as to his guilt.

Social welfare refers to all the services churches or Christians render to assist the victims of social problems. It includes medical clinics, tutoring classes, rescue missions, premarital counseling, flood relief, and a host of other expressions of Christian compassion.

Social action goes farther. It aims to correct the social and political structures and processes of a society that cause the problems. It seeks to exercise political power within a government or, perhaps, to overthrow the government and install a different or purged form of rule.

Most evangelical Christians believe that Christians should have social concern and should engage in social welfare. The problem comes with social action. Should the church engage in social action? If not the church, how about Christian people as participating individuals?

Three positions on social action now exist among evangelical Christians. Some say the exercise of power in politics—political office or political resistance to a government—excludes the true Christian, who is called to suffer, not rule.

Others say the church cannot engage in politics lest its true mission be subverted. "My kingdom," said Jesus, "is not of this world" (John 18:36). The concerned individual, however, can participate in politics and ought to. This is the position of many American evangelicals.

Still other Christians say that not only individual Christians but churches should throw themselves into the cause of social justice and direct their energies toward the liberation of the poor and oppressed.

This third position is very difficult in the United States, with its tradition of separation of church and state, but in other nations, especially in Latin America, some evangelical Christians have called the churches to social action; even, if necessary, to revolution.

I suspect that after we have acknowledged the Lordship of Jesus Christ over all of life—as the Apostles did when they told the Jewish court, "We ought to obey God rather than man" (Acts 5:29)—we will have to resist the temptation to tell other Christians and the churches how to express their obedience to Christ in their unique political situations. Social action is not an area where we find ready answers to complex problems.

Culture

The mission of the church raises other questions about churches' relationship to culture. This is a special concern for missionaries, evangelists, and national leaders in countries where the Gospel has recently been planted. It is also a concern to those in the United States who are working within a subculture such as urban blacks, migrating Hispanos, and even suburban youth.

Culture, in mission circles, does not refer to upper-class people who get their pictures in the paper when they attend the symphony. Culture, as we are using the word, points to man's life in the world, regardless of class. The term represents the corporate ideas and emotions which influence groups of people. It designates a people's links with the past (traditions) and their desires to express themselves not only in abstract ideas but especially in their material creations. Language and customs are usually two of the more obvious expressions of culture.

This means that attendance at the opera may be a true expression of culture for some people, but screaming at a soccer game or betting at a cockfight are just as much a part of another people's way of life.

The problem of culture and the mission of the church arises when we ask what changes in their ways of life the Gospel brings to a people. If a certain people believe that Christians are out to destroy their traditional society, they are likely to lash out in irrational anger. We can find examples of this in the New Testament.

The Jews accused Stephen of teaching "that this Jesus of Nazareth will . . . change the customs which Moses delivered to us" (NIV). And some merchants of Philippi charged Paul and Silas with "disturbing our city" because "they advocate customs which it is not lawful for us Romans to accept or practice" (Acts 6:14, and 16:20-21, RSV). In both cases, one Jewish and the other Roman, the issue concerned customs, either the abandonment of old customs or the introduction of new ones. Culture is expressed by our customs, and people feel threatened when their customs are disturbed.

Is this all that Christians can expect? Since Jesus Christ demands that the whole of life be brought under His control, must the church always oppose existing culture and face the hostility of the world? Many Christians have argued this way and many missions have labored under this assumption.

Other missionary leaders have raised questions about this approach to evangelism and church planting. Just as Jesus' own mission involved His acceptance of the customs and traditions of first-century Judaism, the church today faces the necessity of identifying with the way of life practiced by those it seeks to win.

That is well and good for simple matters like chopsticks, silverware, and finger food but what about those customs and practices that express the religious beliefs of a people? What about ancestor worship or sexual initiation rites? Aren't these opposed to the Christian faith? Can't we carry identification too far and lose Christianity's message in the tribal customs of a region?

These are difficult questions to answer and Christians often disagree on just where the line should be drawn on a host of cultural practices. It seems best to admit that man's culture can be for God, it can be neutral, or it can be against God.

The Lausanne Covenant expressed it this way: "Because man is God's creature, some of his culture is rich in beauty and goodness. Because he has fallen, all of it is tainted with sin and some of it is demonic. Culture, therefore, must always be tested and judged by Scripture."

The church needs the discernment of the Holy Spirit to decide between what may be retained and what must be renounced. Christians who cut free entirely from their society may find themselves rootless and insecure. But Christians who never question their culture may find themselves enslaved to custom rather than the love of Christ.

The Church and the State

The final problem arising from the broad question of the mission of the church is the church's relation to the state. Most Christians today—even Roman Catholics after Vatican II—would support the policy of religious freedom. So we should ask, why?

Religious liberty is the freedom to profess a faith different from that of the dominant religion in a state and to unite in public worship with others who share this faith. This kind of freedom must be distinguished from toleration of religious differences. Mere toleration presumes to grant something that is not rightfully due. Out of a spirit of generosity and from a position of superiority, toleration grants a privilege to an inferior. Religious liberty, however, insists that there are no superior or inferior persons. Before the law, all are equally free.

Religious liberty, we should stress, says nothing about the truth of positions in God's sight. Being a political provision, it is not concerned with questions of religious truth; it only guarantees the opportunity to every man to seek the truth and to assemble with others in quest of it.

Christians, then, holding that God has revealed to man divine truth concerning his salvation, will distinguish what is right before the law and what is true before God. Religious liberty is simply the political context that allows a man to make his choice for or against Jesus Christ under nothing other than moral constraint.

This view is so widely accepted that most Americans think it strange that it was ever denied a person. But for centuries men believed that religious liberty would only lead to social and political chaos. Religion, and at times the Christian religion, served as a social cement binding empires or states together, and persecution of dissenting minorities was acceptable. Even the Protestant Reformers considered religious liberty a threat to a stable society. It fell to the Anabaptists on the European continent and to the Baptists in England to assert first the rights of every man to think and believe according to his own conscience. By the time of the American Revolution many men, Christian and non-Christian, had come to agree.

The bases of religious liberty rest on the New Testament. They do not begin with man as a creature enlightened by reason and able therefore to take his place in a society where intelligent persons concede to others the rights of free discussion. They begin with man as we see him in terms of Jesus Christ and the Gospel.

In the New Testament, man is a being of infinite worth, with rights of personality conferred upon him by God. He is not a thing, a pawn in some politician's game, a cog in an industrial machine, or a number in a computer-controlled state. He is a man, God-created and God-redeemed. Therefore he must be respected by other men and the state.

Christ, as the Gospels disclose, assumed that man was free to choose his destiny, but the Lord preached that man, to be man in the fullest sense, must choose the freedom guaranteed by faith in Him. While man in one sense can be called a free being, in another sense he must experience the liberating power of the Gospel before he can find "the glorious liberty of the children of God" (Rom. 8:21, RSV). The final freedom is from sin and death and hell, but in order to make the decision to follow Christ, man must be free from external constraints, from religious states and state religions. That is how Gospel freedom requires religious freedom.

Another biblical truth supporting religious freedom springs from the nature of the church. The church must be a fellowship of believers who have personally and freely responded to the Gospel invitation. A true family of God simply cannot be created by force. Only a society, therefore, that allows men to decide freely to follow Christ is in harmony with the purposes of the Gospel.

The main point is not the form of government but the way it functions regarding religion. The state and the church have two different responsibilities and two different kinds of authority. Each must seek to achieve the ends which it desires by the means proper to itself. When the state acts as an agent for religious purposes or the church acts as an agent for state purposes, uniformity is gained at the price of liberty. Even American Christians must recognize that an absolute separation of church and state is unrealistic. This would be possible only if the church existed in a realm where the government never functioned. But churches, we know, enjoy police and fire protection; their meeting places are subject to regulations of building codes; and they may be sued in civil courts.

By separation of church and state, we mean that the government should exercise its authority only in civil affairs, not in religious matters. On the other hand, no religion ought to be established by legal grants, advantages, or privileges from the government. God alone is Lord of the conscience.

12

The Destiny of the Church

It looked like Saturday morning TV time at the VanPelt household. Lucy and Linus were sitting in front of the set when she said to Linus, "Go get me a glass of water."

Linus looked surprised. "Why should I do anything for you?" he said. "You never do anything for me."

"On your 75th birthday," Lucy promised, "I'll bake you a cake."

Linus got up, headed for the kitchen, and said, "Life is more pleasant when you have something to look forward to." Well, it is, isn't it?

We must not conclude this study of the church without stressing that the best is yet to come. The crowning explanation of the people of God lies beyond history. There is no scriptural justification for Christians expecting complete fulfillment in this life. Our present experience of salvation in Christ, however genuine and wonderful, is nevertheless incomplete. We still live in bodies subject to decay. We still have by natural birth a sinful nature. And we still live in a world rushing from crime to crime.

The New Testament teaches that the Old Testament saints could not be made perfect without New Testament Christians (Heb. 11:39-40). In the same way, the church on earth is incomplete without the full company and communion of all the saints. In the crowning fulfillment which our Lord foretold, we must "sit down with Abraham, and Isaac, and Jacob" (Matt. 8:11). All of God's people—in the Old Covenant and in the New—must gather "before the throne, and before the Lamb," an innumerable multitude "of all nations, and kindreds, and people and tongues" (Rev. 7:9).

What Is Heaven Like?

The ultimate destiny of the church is the eternal presence of God. The Bible and Christian doctrine call this heaven. What is heaven like? When people ask what Christians believe about heaven, it is not possible to give a precise and detailed answer. The reasons are fairly obvious. How could you explain to a primitive tribesman what life in Los Angeles is like? Yet both Bushmen and Californians live on planet earth, breathe the same air, and enjoy the same sun. But heaven, whatever it is, must be fundamentally different. By definition it must be almost beyond human comprehension.

The most important thing we can say is that heaven is where God is. In terms of the Book of Revelation, "The dwelling of God is with men" (Rev. 21:3, RSV). The climax of the biblical story of God's redemption is "the Holy City," God with His people. In such a community, God will wipe away every tear, and abolish pain, sorrow, and death, "for the former things are passed away" (Rev. 21:4).

Some Christians try to picture the future life much as they do life here and now. And that creates problems. Jesus never spoke of the life to come in strictly literal terms. And apocalyptic writings like the Book of Revelation were never intended to be read as scientific accounts of earthly events. We should never treat allegorical and metaphorical language in this unimaginative way.

The church's future will not be in a space-time environment. As the Bible describes heaven, it simply does not fit our chronology. It is not in time, and the whole idea of calculating years and hours in heaven is like trying to measure love with a steel tape. It simply will not submit to that kind of description.

Any thought of timelessness bothers many people. There is

something decidedly unattractive to human minds about the idea of anything going on for ever and ever. "I'd be bored stiff," people say. "After a few thousand years you'd have done it all." Such people make heaven sound like a rainy day in Hoboken.

Other people are repelled by ideas of playing harps on clouds "up there." But our ideas of space do not fit heaven any better than our ideas of time. Heaven is not "up." This may come as a surprise to some people, because if an idea is old enough, no matter how thin its foundation, it is hard to demolish it. This is particularly true if biblical language seems to support it. For example, the term *ascension*, "going up," to describe the return of Jesus to heaven suggests that God is up there. The view of the universe held by many ancient people seems to have been an earth beneath (and waters "under the earth") with the firmament above, and heaven high above all. But in a remarkable way, various biblical writers at different times put the whole idea of heaven in a totally nonmaterial, nonspatial and nontemporal setting.

In his helpful little book, *Hereafter: What Happens After Death?* author David Winter argues that it isn't necessary to think of heaven up there in strictly literal terms. "Up," he says, "may be used to describe something which is superior to another. Our normal use of the word *higher* illustrates this. We speak of higher rank or higher skills. We don't mean *upward* in terms of physical height; we mean the skills are superior. Heaven is certainly up in that sense. It is infinitely above anything we know. But it is not up geographically. After all, what is up in the United States is down in New Zealand. Heaven is different and it is greatly superior to anything we know on earth, but it is not up there, or even out there" (Wheaton: Harold Shaw, 1972, pp. 73-74).

Neither is heaven necessarily a place with literal golden streets and gates of pearl. In the terms of their day, these were symbols which simply represented the ultimate in beauty and enjoyment. Modern people may speak of a land of endless sunshine and entertaining music. So, deprived of the categories which enable us to describe anything in normal terms—time, space, location—

Christians are usually reduced to saying what heaven is *like*—a technique Jesus Himself used on many occasions.

Heaven is in many respects like God. It is eternal. It is full of beauty, truth, and goodness. But it is not just a list of attributes. It is a way of life. Relationships are important there. We can grow in the truth and experience love as never before. "Now I know in part; then I shall understand fully," says the apostle. "Love never ends" (1 Cor. 13:8, 12, RSV).

The heavens of materialistic religions (such as the Elysian fields of the Romans) are little more than glamorized re-creations of life on earth. On the other hand, the heavens of the Eastern religions, like *Nirvana,* are little more than concepts—they hardly involve living in any ordinary sense of the word.

The Christian heaven, however, avoids both of these extremes. It is not a new season of earthly existence, improved mainly by the absence of certain serious handicaps, such as pain and death; but neither is it simply a concept. In heaven, God's own will lives, and lives more fully and satisfyingly than ever before. And that life will involve all the really important elements of what we know as life: corporate fellowship, personal development, increasing knowledge, and heart-to-heart communication. All of these are possible because life in heaven will be like life on earth in one important respect: personality will be expressed through a body. The differences in existence are enormous, but the quality of life retains this key similarity to earth. We shall recognize other saints and our loved ones more by who they are than by what they look like—but we shall know them with a depth of love unimaginable in our present human existence. Life will be transformed in the presence of the Creator and Sustainer of eternal happiness.

This link with earthly life is important. Heaven develops out of earth. Human personality flowers there into its most wonderful form and the Sun of Righteousness is the personality of Christ. This is how the Apostle John put it: "We are God's children now; it does not yet appear what we shall be, but we know that when He appears we shall be like Him, for we shall see Him as He is" (1 John 3:2, RSV). That is the church's destiny in heaven—

to be like Christ: not Christ limited, as He was on earth, to the confines of time and flesh, but Christ risen, the free, timeless Christ of Easter morning. That, in a sentence, is what we shall be like in heaven; and a community of people like that is what heaven will be.

Who Goes to Heaven?

If we grant that there is a heaven to which it is possible to go after death, who goes there? Everybody? Or just some people? And if only some, why are others excluded? Obviously, these questions have been raised over and over again, throughout human history. Surprisingly, almost all known religions have settled for what is, on the face of it, the less attractive line of thinking: that admission to heaven is by selection and that the selection is based on moral considerations. In Christian terms, that means there is a final judgment.

David Winter advances an argument for the idea of judgment after death that is, I think, highly persuasive. It depends upon this basic premise: that there is a God and that He is good. If we reject that idea, then we have no firm reason for believing in any kind of moral judgment after death. But if we do accept the idea that a God of goodness exists, then the logic of the case for a judgment to come is almost irresistible.

Few would deny that life in this world is unjust. The rich exploit the poor, the ruthless terrorize the humble, and the powerful abuse the weak. Lovable children are denied a stable home and capable couples are unable to have children. Tyrants die peacefully in their beds while saints sometimes pass in agony to the stake.

Clearly, man knows no universal justice on Planet Earth. The most massive injustices go unpunished, and the most admirable unselfishness goes unrewarded.

Yet the instinct of justice remains strong in all of us. One of the first things a child learns to say is, "It's not fair." We spend our years appealing to some abstract principle of justice that we feel in our bones and assume that everyone else also feels. Nationality, politics, and culture make no difference. Communists, atheists, humanists, and Christians make the same appeal: "It's not fair." And yet we all recognize that, in the final analysis, this life is not fair. With the best intentions in the world, human justice is fallible.

If—as we are assuming—there is a God who is almighty and good, how can He possibly allow this pervasive injustice to continue? If He does nothing, either now or after this life, to correct this gross unfairness and dethrone the reign of evil, He is either not all-powerful (and so cannot do it) or He is not good (and so does not care). But if He is all-powerful and good—which is what the word *God* means to most of us—then it seems He must act to put things right. Justice on a cosmic scale must prevail and must be seen to prevail, or God is not God.

Obviously, God has not yet established justice on earth. So the strong presumption is that He will establish it after this life is over. And that is what the Bible teaches: "It is appointed for men to die once, and after that comes judgment" (Heb. 9:27, RSV). (See David Winter, *Hereafter,* pp. 82-85.)

The theme of the final judgment of God, in which the mighty are dethroned, the proud are scattered in the imagination of their hearts, the rich sent empty away, and the good who are hungry and poor are exalted, runs strongly through the teaching of Jesus and the Apostles (Luke 1:51-53). We might think that God is blind to human injustice, but one day mankind will see that He cares intensely about it, and the inequalities and evils of life on earth will be put right.

Henry Wadsworth Longfellow affirmed the triumph of divine justice in those familiar lines about Christmas' meaning:

I heard the bells on Christmas day
Their old familiar carols play,
And wild and sweet the words repeat
Of peace on earth, goodwill to men.

And in despair I bowed my head:
"There is no peace on earth," I said.
"For hate is strong, and mocks the song
Of peace on earth, goodwill to men."

Then pealed the bells more loud and deep:
"God is not dead, nor doth He sleep;
The wrong shall fail, the right prevail,
With peace on earth, goodwill to men."

A vital part of this process is a final judgment after death. Jesus described it in terms of a shepherd separating the sheep from the goats (Matt. 25:32). However much it may offend liberal sentiment, the Bible indicates that Jesus believed and taught that people could be excluded from heaven. The reason for this is quite simple. Heaven is a community of total goodness. It is life eternal in the presence of God. To allow evil into heaven would be like dropping a rotten potato into a ten-pound bag of good ones: the place would no longer be totally good, and would soon become totally evil. All impurity and sin will be excluded from heaven, so that it may be heaven: "Nothing unclean shall enter it, nor any one who practices abomination or falsehood, but only those who are written in the Lamb's book of life" (Rev. 21:27, RSV).

But in that case we may ask, "Who can possibly hope to get to heaven? Where is the person good enough to live in a community of total goodness, without spoiling it? Isn't God going to be lonely, living in the isolation of His own holiness, while all His self-centered and morally corrupt creatures are excluded?"

The answer to that question lies in the last phrase of Revelation 21:27. Those who enter heaven have their names written in the "Lamb's book of life." They are members of a "great multitude which no man could number, from every nation, from all tribes and people and tongues . . . who have washed their robes and made them white in the blood of the Lamb" (Rev. 7:9, 14, RSV).

The Lamb is, of course, Jesus Christ, and the reference to His blood is to His sacrifice on the cross, where He died for the forgiveness of men's sins. Through that spotless offering, Christians believe, it is possible for ordinary men and women, fallible and faulty as we all are, to be forgiven and reconciled to God. In the peculiar imagery of the Book of Revelation, their names are written in the Lamb's book of life.

They will go to heaven, not on their own merits, but on those of Jesus Christ because He has died for their sins. That is the Christian Gospel. It is God's way of keeping heaven holy and yet admitting to it people no better than we are.

So the short answer to the question, "Who goes to heaven?" is: those whose sins have been forgiven through the sacrifice of Jesus Christ. And that means that heaven in this sense can begin now. Eternal life is something that mortals can know in this life. Christians in every age have testified of eternity already in their hearts. And that is the best possible preparation for the moment of death, whenever it comes to us. As Paul puts it, "For to me to live is Christ, and to die is gain" (Phil. 1:21). If eternal life means living with Christ, then death must be gain because it will mean a closer relationship with Him, with all the barriers of mortality and sin removed.

For the church, the fellowship of forgiven sinners, death is not the end. It is not the end of life, or love, or beauty. It is not the end of anything good, worthwhile, or lovely. It is not the end of those we love in Christ, nor is it the end of our own spiritual and moral development. "Like sailors looking out over the water," says David Winter, "we can only see as far as the horizon that men call death. But beyond that horizon lies more, so much more; hidden from our eyes, but revealed, item by item, to our minds and our hearts by faith" (*Hereafter*, p. 91).

How Is the Church Made Ready?

When the Lord Jesus reappears He will complete His victory by triumphing over the last enemy, death, and by giving to all His people glorified resurrection bodies. In His own resurrection from the grave as the triumphant Man, He was the firstfruits of the final harvest. Then, "At His coming they that are Christ's" will also be raised or transfigured to share His glory. So Paul, the Apostle, wrote: "But our citizenship is in heaven. And we eagerly await a Saviour from there, the Lord Jesus Christ, who, by the power that enables Him to bring everything under His control, will transform our lowly bodies so that they will be like His glorious body" (Phil. 3:20-21, NIV).

The Apostle also explained that the generation of Christians who are alive on the earth when this occurs will not die, but will simultaneously share in the same bodily glorification. This glorification is necessary, because our present corruptible bodies of flesh and blood cannot inherit the incorruptible kingdom of God. So Paul declared: "Listen, I tell you a mystery: We shall not all sleep, but we shall all be changed—in a flash, in the twinkling of an eye, at the last trumpet. For the trumpet will sound, the dead will be raised imperishable, and we shall be changed. For the perishable must clothe itself with the imperishable, and the mortal with immortality" (1 Cor. 15:51-53, NIV).

The relation of the resurrection body to our present body is one of continuity and transformation. In 1 Corinthians 15:35-38 and 42-44, Paul compares the body to a seed which is transformed into a flower. It is sown in one state but it blooms forth in another—continuity but wonderful transformation. The best illustration of the change, however, is the risen Lord Jesus. He was different. The two who walked the Emmaus Road with Him did not recognize Him. Yet, when He took bread to break it, He was known to them in the breaking of bread (Luke 24:30-31).

The completion of redemption calls for a change in the bodies of those who are on earth when Jesus returns. And it means that the departed saints, who have left their earthly bodies behind them here in the grave, will be provided new glorified bodies like the Lord's. The living and the once dead will be caught up from the earth to meet the Lord in the air, and to be forever with Him. Again, to quote Paul: "For the Lord Himself will come down from heaven, with a loud command, with the voice of the archangel and with the trumpet call of God, and the dead in Christ will rise first. After that, we who are still alive and are left will be caught up with them in the clouds to meet the Lord in the air. And so we will be with the Lord forever" (1 Thes. 4:16-17, NIV).

In my files, I have a simple mimeographed piece of paper. It is dated April 6, Friday, 1973. There is a story behind this piece of paper. The mother of a girl in a Bible class I taught had been taken to the hospital in September for what everyone thought was to be simple surgery. But upon cutting into Mrs. Griffith, the doctors discovered that she had cancer. It had spread so far that the surgeon could do nothing for her. She was repaired surgically and sent home. I shall never forget her testimony at Thanksgivingtime. Like many churches, our Thanksgiving service is a time of sharing. Mrs. Griffith stood, and in a moving way, in spite of this tragedy, told the church that her expectations were unto Christ.

During those months between October and April when she died, Mrs. Griffith read her Bible a great deal and collected a number of verses which moved her and were the basis of her hope. She also gathered a number of quotations and poems. The paper in my file is a copy of her notes and underlined verses in her Bible.

She wrote, "We cannot always be sure of God's ways of dealing with us but if we could, we wouldn't need to exercise faith." Among the many verses she had copied and underscored were 2 Corinthians 4:17-18: "Our light affliction, which is but for a moment, worketh for us a far more exceeding and eternal weight of glory; while we look not at the things which are seen but at the things which are not seen: for the things which are seen are temporal, but the things which are not seen are eternal." And then she wrote,

Nothing can go beyond His love
In earth beneath, in heaven above.
The passing hour may evil seem
But love at last will reign supreme.

Mrs. Griffith believed that Jesus Christ is coming again and that on that day of resurrection, death will be "swallowed up in victory."

The magnificent event of the second coming of Christ will terminate the hope of the church on earth. But until that hour arrives, Scripture directs us to fill our eyes with the expectation of that great day. The concluding verses of Dean Alford's great hymn, "Ten Thousand Times Ten Thousand," catch exactly the biblical anticipation of the reunion of all God's people at the return of Christ, focusing attention at last on the supreme cause of the joy, Jesus Christ Himself.

Oh, then what raptured greetings
   On Canaan's happy shore,
What knitting severed friendships up
   Where partings are no more:
Then eyes with joy shall sparkle
   That brimmed with tears of late;
Orphans no longer fatherless,
   Nor widows desolate.
Bring near Thy great salvation,
   Thou Lamb for sinners slain;
Fill up the roll of Thine elect,
   Then take Thy power and reign;
Appear, Desire of Nations,
   Thine exiles long for home;
Show in the heavens Thy promised sign,
   Thou Prince and Saviour, come.

For Further Reading

Flew, R. Newton. *Jesus and His Church: A Study of the Idea of the Ecclesia in the New Testament* (London: Epworth Press, 1956).

Getz, Gene A. *Sharpening the Focus of the Church* (Chicago: Moody Press, 1974).

Griffiths, Michael. *God's Forgetful Pilgrims: Recalling the Church to its Reason for Being* (Grand Rapids: Wm. B. Eerdmans, 1975).

Hort, Fenton John Anthony. *The Christian Ecclesia: A Course of Lectures on the Early History and Early Conceptions of the Ecclesia* (London: Macmillan & Co., 1914).

Newbigin, Lesslie. *The Household of God: Lectures on the Nature of the Church* (New York: Friendship Press, 1954).

Saucy, Robert L. *The Church in God's Program* (Chicago: Moody Press, 1972).

Synder, Howard A. *The Community of the King* (Downers Grove, IL: InterVarsity Press, 1977).

Stibbs, Alan. *God's Church: A Study in the Biblical Doctrine of the People of God* (Downers Grove, IL: InterVarsity Press, 1959).

Stott, John R. W. *Christian Mission in the Modern World* (Downers Grove, IL: InterVarsity Press, 1975).

Trueblood, Elton. *The Incendiary Fellowship* (New York: Harper & Row, 1967).